MEMORY IN «LA CELESTINA»

DOROTHY SHERMAN SEVERIN

MEMORY
IN «LA CELESTINA»

TAMESIS BOOKS LIMITED

LONDON

Colección Támesis

SERIE A - MONOGRAFIAS, XIX

Depósito legal: M. 16.773 - 1970

Printed in Spain by Talleres Gráficos de EDICIONES CASTILLA, S. A.
Maestro Alonso, 23 - Madrid

for

TAMESIS BOOKS LIMITED
LONDON

CONTENTS

FOREWORD

La Celestina *has been the subject of such extensive literary criticism in nearly five hundred years of existence that any new study must of necessity focus on a specific characteristic of the work. In this book, originally presented as a dissertation at Harvard University, I have undertaken to examine Fernando de Rojas' manipulation of memory in* La Celestina *as a literary device and his understanding of memory as a human function. This line of literary investigation was first suggested to me by my supervisor at Harvard, Stephen Gilman. My thanks are due to him for his guidance in the preparation of this study, also to the Woodrow Wilson Foundation for financial assistance in the form of a Dissertation Fellowship. I would also like to express my gratitude to Alan Deyermond of Westfield College, University of London, who was kind enough to comment on and suggest alterations for the published version.*

ABBREVIATIONS

BAE	*Biblioteca de Autores Españoles.*
BHS	*Bulletin of Hispanic Studies.*
CL	*Comparative Literature.*
HR	*Hispanic Review.*
PMLA	*Publications of the Modern Language Association of America.*
PQ	*Philological Quarterly.*
RAE	Real Academia Española.
RF	*Romanische Forschungen.*
RFE	*Revista de Filología Española.*
RFH	*Revista de Filología Hispánica.*
SBE	Sociedad de Bibliófilos Españoles.

I. INTRODUCTION

In the lovers' dialogue from Act XII of his *La Celestina* or the *Tragicomedia de Calisto y Melibea,* Fernando de Rojas reaches the climax of a long development in the reexamination and redefinition of memory in the work. For here, in the first colloquy of the lovers in Melibea's garden, memory is implicitly defined as the whole of consciousness, after eleven earlier *autos* which have gradually transformed the idea of memory from its traditional material rôle to this new state.

Yet it is typical of Rojas that he should have cloaked this literary innovation in the protective coloring of literary tradition and commonplace, for Calisto's revelations are expressed in terms of the «awakening of love» topic — «hasta que ya los rayos ylustrantes de tu muy claro gesto dieron luz en mis ojos...»:

> CALISTO: ...O quántos días antes de agora passados me fue venido este pensamiento a mi coraçón, *e por impossible le rechaçaua de mi memoria,* hasta que ya los rayos ylustrantes de tu muy claro gesto dieron luz en mis ojos, encendieron mi coraçón, despertaron mi lengua, estendieron mi merecer, acortaron mi couardía, destorcieron mi encogimiento, doblaron mis fuerças, desadormescieron mis pies e manos, finalmente, me dieron tal osadía, que me han traydo con su mucho poder a este sublimado estado en que agora me veo, oyendo de grado tu suaue voz. La qual, si ante de agora no conociese e no sintiesse tus saludables olores, no podría creer que careciessen de engaño tus palabras. Pero, como soy cierto de tu limpieza de sangre e fechos, me estoy remirando si soy yo Calisto, a quien tanto bien se le haze.

> MELIBEA: Señor Calisto, tu mucho merecer, tus estremadas gracias, tu alto nascimiento han obrado que, después que de ti houe entera noticia, ningún momento de mi coraçón te partiesses.

E avnque muchos días he pugnado por lo dissimular, no he podido tanto que, *en tornándome aquella muger tu dulce nombre
a la memoria,* no descubriesse mi desseo e viniesse a este lugar
e tiempo, donde te suplico ordenes e dispongas de mi persona
segund querrás (II, 85-86, Act XII). [1]

Nevertheless, both Calisto and Melibea acknowledge in their
colloquy that memory has taken on strange powers — that it has
become equated with human experience. The past in memory collides
with the present; «E aunque muchos días he pugnado por lo dissimular, no he podido tanto que, en tornándome aquella muger tu
dulce nombre a la memoria, no descubriesse mi desseo e viniesse a este
lugar e tiempo...» This acute time-consciousness in the characters
of *La Celestina,* this realization that the past, present, and future
are bound together with iron links of causality, is a primary literary
innovation of the work. And the use of *memoria* as the verbal
symbol for human consciousness of time, is nothing short of a re-
volution in meaning. Through this redefinition of memory, *La Celestina* becomes a work distinguished by its artistic exploitation of
memory, not as an idea, but as a vital part of human experience.

Although a great deal of work has been done in recent criticism

---

[1] I am using for page references the standard critical edition of Julio Cejador
y Frauca in *Clásicos Castellanos* 20, 23 (Madrid, 1962; first ed. 1910), but have
corrected it against my own text in the Alianza Editorial series (Madrid, 1969) and
M. Criado de Val and G. D. Trotter's critical edition (Madrid, 1958). Although
the latter uses an unreliable Seville «1502» edition of the expanded twenty-one
act *Tragicomedia,* as its textual base, it does have the advantage of giving the
only complete list of variants in the Burgos 1499 and Seville 1501 editions of
the primitive sixteen-act *Comedia.* Cejador's careless edition is, however, based
on the more authentic Valencia 1514 edition. For a dating on typographical
evidence of the so-called 1502 editions, see F. J. Norton's *Printing in Spain 1501-
1520* (Cambridge, England, 1966). For a list of editions of *La Celestina,* their
contents, and their present location, see Simón Díaz, *Bibliografía de la literatura
hispánica* III (2nd edition, vol. II, Madrid, 1965), 4784-4970, and Clara Louisa
Penney, *The book called Celestina in the Library of the Hispanic Society of America*
(New York, 1954). The italics in the extract quoted above are mine. I have not
indicated the *Tragicomedia* interpolation in the primitive *Comedia* text; when
this information is relevant, it will be mentioned separately. Rojas' alterations
in the text have, however, been indicated in square brackets. Page references
are to the volume and page of Cejador's two-volume edition, with Act references
where this is not obvious from the context. The exception to this rule is the chapter
on «Time and Character», in which the numerous short references bear no indi-
cation of the Act in which they appear. In quotes from early printings I have
supplied modern accentuation but generally retained original punctuation, mod-
ifying it only where the reading would otherwise be obscure.

on the question of time in *La Celestina*, [2] memory has remained only a peripheral topic of investigation. The possibility that memory in *La Celestina* might be a field ripe for investigation was first suggested by Stephen Gilman, in an article on the *Lazarillo:*

> In *La Celestina* the nameless city fills with society, events, and artefacts only when remembered. During the rest of the time the intensely present dialogue eliminates everything that is non-essential to the situation of the speakers. But the *Lazarillo,* being all memory, confirms Lukacs' intuition that the novel, as a genre of experience, depends first of all on memory for its joining of inner and outer worlds. [3]

But to undertake an investigation of Rojas' understanding and use of memory in *La Celestina,* it is necessary to approach the topic from both the internal and external angles. For the internal workings of memory in *La Celestina* must be considered in the light of character development and human consciousness in the work and also as an approach to the reexamination of the problem of time in *La Celestina*. The «external» considerations involve the relationship between memory in *La Celestina* and memory in previous and later fictional genres. Then too there is the related question as to whether memory might not provide a third-person corrective to the dialogic situation of *La Celestina*.

To approach these topics with some degree of logical order, it is necessary to begin by showing how the author of the first act, the «primitive author», [4] sets a style and a precedent for the function of memory in the work. It may then perhaps be demonstrated that Rojas takes up and develops this theme, using the differences of their memories as a device to illustrate differences between the personae; and, with great skill, employs Celestina herself as the critical catalyst in this process. At this level, therefore, a detailed examination of the various forms of memory displayed by the characters may provide us with some additional insight into the personae themselves. But because memory in *La Celestina* may also serve a wider purpose, one

---

[2]   See below, p. 43.

[3]   «The Death of Lazarillo de Tormes», *PMLA* LXXXI (1966), 156, n. 32.

[4]   I defer to the prevailing critical opinion that Rojas was telling the truth when he claimed to have found the first act. See Martín de Riquer in *RFE* XLI (1957), 373-395 («Fernando de Rojas y el primer acto de 'La Celestina'») for the most documented support of the «primitive author» theory.

should also consider the relationship between memory and the plot of Rojas' work. Here, I hope, it will be possible to show that memory is not only an agent, along with others, impelling the characters towards their deaths, but that it provides a sense of continuity and consistency to the overall structure of *La Celestina.* This latter function, however, turns upon the interaction of memory and time within the work, and for this reason I propose to reexamine the thorny question of time in *La Celestina,* approaching the problem on this occasion from the angle of memory and Rojas' scholastic heritage.

The over-all purpose of this study, however, is to demonstrate how memory plays an integral part in Rojas' concept of human life; how each person is revealed through memory, thus divulging his innermost character. Rojas' characters are the sum of their past and present, and life and memory become synonymous in *La Celestina.*

A. Memory: The Tradition

As a vantage point from which to view the extent of Rojas' innovations in the area of memory, it is useful to enumerate in brief the various scholastic traditions of memory which would have influenced Rojas in his own time. According to one strongly held theory, memory belonged to the quintet of internal senses or wits: memory, estimation, imagination, fantasy and common sense. [5] Yet as Frances A. Yates has demonstrated, [6] the medieval mind also drew upon the *Rhetorica ad Herennium* for a second classification of memory as a part of rhetoric. [7] The prologue to *La Celestina* shows that this rhetorical definition was never far from Rojas' mind, for he states: «Pero aquéllos para cuyo verdadero placer es todo, desechan el cuento de la hystoria para contar, coligen la suma para su prouecho, ríen lo donoso, las sentencias e dichos de philósophos guardan en su memoria para trasponer en lugares conuenibles a sus autos e propósitos» (I. 24). That Rojas here acknowledges the debt

---

[5]   See C. S. Lewis, *The Discarded Image* (Cambridge, 1964), pp. 161-162.

[6]   *The Art of Memory* (London, 1966).

[7]   «Rhetoric as an art *(ars)* has five divisions: *inventio... dispositio... elocutio... memoria... actio...*» E. R. Curtius, *European Literature and the Latin Middle Ages* (New York, 1963), p. 68.

4

to the Ciceronian rhetorical dichotomy —memory of «words» (*verba* «las sentencias e dichos»); and «things» (*res* «el cuento...la suma»)[8]— is evident, though it is also significant to note that the formal definition is colored by the individual personalities of his readers. Some, not all, will choose to memorize useful passages, «para trasponer...a sus autos e propósitos». As we shall see, Rojas' predilection is for the «res» — those personal memories of the past which go into the mental constitution of his characters. The third and last of the common medieval memory traditions was the Thomist doctrine which Christianized the rhetorical art of memory and linked it with Prudence. Rojas would have known of this view through his acquaintance with Petrarch's *De remediis utriusque fortunae.*[9]

As an illustration of how Rojas manages to combine and transform the rhetorical and Christian traditions of memory, we may take one short example from the penultimate act of *La Celestina,* without encroaching too far upon our examination of memory in the work. Melibea, speaking to her father before her suicide, refers to «algunas consolatorias palabras ... coligidas e sacadas de aquellos antigos libros que tú, por más aclarar mi ingenio, me mandauas leer» (II. 198, Act XX). Seemingly, the reference is to the formal Ciceronian memory of «words» —the aphorisms of the ancients— as opposed to personal memory. But personal memory is involved as well, for these few words also suggest the intense personal relationship which has existed between the aged father and his only child. By the end of

---

[8]   This would remain common doctrine throughout the sixteenth century. Luis Vives included it in his *De anima et vita* (Basel, 1538): «Nec memoriam habent cmnes pariter ad omnia, sunt qui uerba, sunt qui res meminerunt facilius» (p. 56). Vives too could not avoid adapting the formal definition to individual personality.

[9]   GAU. Memoria apprime tenax est. RA. Vnde haec igitur obliuio caelestium preceptorum, quae tam pauca sunt numero. Vnde obliuio dei unius. Vnde obliuio suimet. GAU. Memoria admodum tenax est. RA. Terrenarum et inutilium rerum credo: quonam vero et quo uaga haec volatilisque memoria; quae cum caelum: terramque peragrauerit in seipsam nesciens reuerti: quod unum necessarium: ac salubre erat: obliuiscitur.» *Clarissimi de Remediis utriusque fortunae: ad Azonam* (Cremona, 1492), fols. Avii, viii. A contemporary Spanish translation renders the Latin thus:
GOZO: Es mi memoria muy tenaz. RAZON. ¿Pues de dó viene tanto oluido de los diuinos preceptos que en número son muy pocos: de dó el de Dios que es vno; y de dó el de ty mesmo? GOZO. Es mi memoria muy tenaz. RAZON. De las terrenales e inútiles cosas bien lo creo. Dónde se espacia esta vuestra veloz memoria: que después que ha trascorrido el cielo y la tierra: no sabiendo tornar ensí se oluida delo que le era nescessario y saludable... (*De los remedios contra prospera y aduersa fortuna,* Valladolid, Diego de Gumiel, 1510, fols. Bviii, Ci.) For a thorough investigation of the influence of Petrarch in *La Celestina,* see A. D. Deyermond, *The Petrarchan Sources of La Celestina* (Oxford, 1961).

La Celestina, as we shall see, apparently mechanical memory evokes a past of human experience and companionship. But Melibea's reminiscence also contains overtones of the Christian idea of memory as a prudent defense against causality, a way to enlighten the mind with the lessons of the past — «Por más aclarar mi ingenio». And this, in turn, becomes the ultimate irony of Rojas' approach to memory. For in *La Celestina* there is no defense against the fatal powers of the past in the present. Death will overtake all the characters, whether or not they obey the warnings of memory, and Pleberio, the most prudent, will in the end suffer most cruelly.

B. «LA CELESTINA», MEMORY, AND LITERARY PRECEDENT

In future chapters we will be considering Rojas' (and the primitive author's) development of a literary style for memory, and the gradual integration of memory and character. For the moment, however, let us enter the area of literary history in order to analyze the innovation of Rojas' approach to memory. In terms of literary history, Rojas has been presented by critics as the man who solved the problems of voice posed by medieval Spanish literature. The *Libro de Buen Amor* introduced the problem of the fluid *yo;* [10] that is to say, the narrative first person of the *Libro de Buen Amor* is not a stable autobiographical entity, but a fluid 'self' which Juan Ruiz injects into various situations, as Don Melón, etc. To this the Arcipreste de Talavera added the fluid *tú;* a 'second-person' presence which in fact is generalized and archetypal: the woman whose chicken was stolen is not a single woman, but is representative of all women who have ever had that experience. Rojas essentially solved these generic dilemmas by creating a vital, two-person dialogic situation. [11]

---

[10] Américo Castro traces the various metamorphoses of the «yo» in Juan Ruiz's work to Arabic influence; «el yo árabe... nunca sería como un proyectil que cruzara el espacio en conflicto con su atmósfera. Insisto en que la literatura árabe carece de drama y de novela porque no cabe en ella la pugna entre un yo y otro yo.» *La realidad histórica de España* (México, 1954), p. 414. For an interpretation of the autobiographical style of the *LBA* as part of European literary tradition, see G. B. Gybbon-Monypenny, «Autobiography in the *Libro de Buen Amor* in the Light of some Literary Comparisons,» *BHS* XXIV (1957), 63-78.

[11] This analysis of the *Corbacho* and *La Celestina* can be found in Gilman, *The Art of «La Celestina»* (Madison, 1956), p. 28. María Rosa Lida de Malkiel disagrees with this agenério analysis of *La Celestina,* and so classifies it as a «come-

But the real generic crisis of Rojas' own time was that of the third person, posed, above all, by that bizarre conglomeration of styles and genres which is known as the Spanish sentimental novel. The narrative schizophrenia of the sentimental novel was conditioned to some extent by its sources. And this crisis seems to have been precipitated by the attempt to combine the first-person memories of *La Fiammetta*[12] with the third-person narration of the *Historia de duobus amantibus,*[13] and with the story-telling techniques of the books of chivalry. Without question the latter belong within Ramón Fernandez' category of the *récit:* «Le roman est la représentation d'événements qui ont lieu dans le temps, représentation soumise aux conditions d'apparition et de développement de ces événements. Le récit est la présentation d'événements qui ont eu lieu, et dont la reproduction est réglée par le narrateur conformément aux lois de l'exposition et de la persuasion.»[14] The problem of

dia humanística», (*La originalidad artística de La Celestina,* Buenos Aires, 1962, pp. 27 ff.). Marcel Bataillon agrees with her analysis of the roots of the book in *La Célestine selon Fernando de Rojas* (Paris, 1961), linking the book with the genre he calls the «Art d'amour», but insisting on the originality of le *genre célestinesque* (pp. 77-78).

[12] Gilman has also analysed the first-person environment of *La Fiammetta:* «in the *Fiammetta,* there is no thematic encounter of human lives in dialogue, nor of duration and dimension in human life... Fiammetta, judged from the theme of *La Celestina,* has been trapped in the second person, and so isolated from the world. A creature of memory in which the *yo* is never actual, she can never find either the facts or the values which might give meaning to her tears», *Art,* pp. 191-192.

[13] Aeneas Sylvius' *Historia de duobus amantibus,* like the books of chivalry, is a *récit* «of which the reproduction is regulated by the narrator in conformity with the laws of exposition and persuasion», but with the distinction of an analysis of consciousness introduced through the letters sent by the lovers. Memory is formalized in the *Historia.* For the writer, the past of his characters does exist, but must be disposed of briefly: «Lucrecia entre aquellas resplandecía, no en hedad de veynte años; dela familia o linaje delos Camillos; casada con Menelao, rico varón: indigno empero: a quien tanta honrra serviesse; antes por cierto merecedor que la muger se tornasse como dizen ciervo» (fols. Aii, Aiii). For the lovers, memory is the formalized medieval memory and forgetfulness caused by love: «Mucho huelgo que mis joyas en qualquier manera ayas rescebido: alguna vez te traerán ala memoria mi amor» (fol. Birecto); «que más me apremias en deuoción de tu prudencia que en oluidança de tu amor» (fol. Biirecto). The attempt to escape the dead hand of a straightforward third-person exposition is never really successful in the *Historia;* Eurialo and Lucrecia never attain the «yo-tú» relationship of awareness of Calisto and Melibea. (I use for purposes of rhetorical comparison an early translation, Seville: Jacobo Cromberger, 1512).

[14] *Messages* (Paris, 1926), p. 60. He expands this statement later on: «Il nous devient aisé maintenant d'opposer au schème du récit pur le schème du roman pur. Le roman trouve sa base et son centre de gravité là où le récit cherche sa confir-

7

third-person narration is most painfully obvious in the first Spanish sentimental novel, Juan del Padrón's *Siervo libre de amor*.[15] The story-within-a-story is so clumsy as to be almost incomprehensible. Diego de San Pedro later formalizes his own approach to the problem of narration, but it is not until the pure epistolary form of Juan de Segura's «Proceso de cartas de amores» that the problem is really solved (or perhaps by-passed) with the removal of the narrative voice.

But this narrative crisis only partly explains the difference between the sentimental novel and the *roman*. It is memory which, according to Georg Lukács, provides the novel with a link between the subjective and objective lives, and which solves the paradox of this duality:

> Nur in dem Roman und in einzelnen, ihm angenäherten, epischen Formen kommt eine schöpferische, den Gegenstand treffende und ihn umwandelnde Erinnerung vor. Das echt Epische dieses Gedächtnisses ist die erlebende Bejahung des Lebensprozesses. Die Dualität von Innerlichkeit and Aussenwelt kann hier für das Subjekt aufgehoben werden, wenn es die organische Einheit seines ganzen Lebens als das Gewachsensein seiner lebendigen Gegenwart aus dem in der Erinnerung zusammengedrängten, vergangenen Lebensstrome erblickt. Die Überwindung der Dualität, also das Treffen und Einbeziehen des Objekts, macht dieses Erlebnis zum Element einer echt epischen Form.[16]

The sentimental novel fails to perceive that memory is the vital bond which ties man to his surroundings, and that this dialogue between subjective and objective worlds lifts the characters of a work above the level of cardboard cutouts manipulated by the author for the amusement and edification of his public.

Diego de San Pedro is the only sentimental novelist who begins to approach this problem of memory — although his narrative is still a clumsy hodge-podge of styles. In the *Tractado de Amores de*

---

mation et sa conclusion: dans l'évocation spontanée et immédiate de la vie morale et physique, dans le cours imprévisible d'une durée psychique ou d'une action... Le roman pur témoigne, soit de la faculté échue à l'auteur de rendre l'atmosphère et les nuances d'une scène imaginaire comme s'il était le spectateur d'une scène réelle, soit de sa faculté de vivre de la vie intérieure d'un personnage que n'est pas lui...» (pp. 63-64).

[15] *Obras de Juan Rodríguez de la Cámara (o del Padrón)*, SBE 22, ed. Antonio Paz y Melia (Madrid, 1884), pp. 35-80.

[16] Georg Lukács, *Die Theorie des Romans* (Berlin: Spandau, 1963), p. 131.

Arnalte y Lucenda, [17] San Pedro adopts the expedient of the story-within-a-story. He, as author, stumbles onto the bleak mansion of Arnalte, who tells San Pedro his sad story. Here the author makes the first concerted effort in Spanish prose fiction to carry the genre beyond the level of the recitation, attempting to enter the lives and thoughts of his characters. His use of memory begins to approach the level of an examination of consciousness, as when he first arrives at Arnalte's house and remarks of it and its color — «E con la memoria de aquello, el trabajo passado y la pena presente oluidada, e por darme priessa para llegar a ella, el espacioso y litigado pensamiento que sobre su color tenía dexé» (p. 5). Nevertheless, San Pedro's use of memory fails to convince, for the author's thoughts are expressed in terms of the allegories of love which so severely limited the originality of the *cancionero*-oriented literati of the fifteenth century. Memory even fails in its third-person function of supplying descriptive background material for the tale — the landscapes are allegorical, and physical appearances are conventional. Diego de San Pedro manages only to lift Spanish prose fiction to a level equivalent to that in other European countries. He fails to transcend the glorified recitation.

San Pedro's *Cárcel de Amor* uses much the same narrative techniques as the *Arnalte.* The significant differences in the later book are in refinement of technique, rather than in new departures. Specifically, the author does not just listen to the hero's story; rather, he becomes personally involved in the exchange of letters, and the epistles carry a much greater burden of the story. There is little interference of extraneous material, the attack on and defense of women being the one notable exception, and the allegorical figures carry a force in the *Cárcel* which they lacked in the *Arnalte,* the obvious example being San Pedro's «wild man». However, here again memory's function is circumscribed by the conventions of love. Memory is one of the four pillars of the prison of love (along with *entendimiento, razón* and *voluntad*), and briefly speaks its set piece: «Pues el Entendimiento y la Razón consienten por que sin morir no pueda ser libre, yo prometo de nunca olvidar» (p. 123).

In summary, therefore, it could be said that Diego de San Pedro is the only sentimental novelist who even begins to face the question

---

[17] See his *Obras,* ed. Samuel Gili y Gaya, Clásicos Castellanos 133 (Madrid, 1950).

of memory as the link between the characters and their surroundings. Juan de Flores bypasses it in order to play with the genre; his *Historia de Grisel y Mirabella* [18] is primarily an imaginative restatement of the fifteenth-century feminist debates, with the literary figures Torrellas and Braçayda as antagonist and advocate of femininity. In *Grimalte y Gradissa* [19] he undertakes to «complete» the *Fiammetta,* and although his ingenious and playful approach to the question of genre sets an intriguing precedent for the future of the Spanish novel; he glosses over the necessity of tackling the problem of memory. The Spanish sentimental romance fails doubly — it fails to solve the problems of narrative voice and of personal voice. It lacks an authentic objective or subjective reality. Clearly, Rojas was familiar with the Spanish sentimental novel. [20] It was the fictional rage of his generation, and presented itself as the easiest target for literary satire in *La Celestina,* as well as supplying a basic plot — the lovers' tragedy. Act VI, Celestina's presentation of Melibea's *cordón* to Calisto, is largely dedicated to a satirical portrait of the overwrought Calisto, representative of the countless Arnaltes of contemporary fiction and poetry. The contempt expressed by the menservants and Celestina («Bien te entiendo, Sempronio. Déjale, que él caerá de su asno, y acaba», I, 228, Act VI) no doubt reflects Rojas' opinion of a genre with so little vitality. And the fact that Calisto is to some extent a satire of a contemporary stereotype explains why he has traditionally been held in low esteem by the critics, and often lacks the vital autonomy of the other characters.

It has been thought that Rojas, like the sentimental novelists, avoided the problem of third-person narration; that his two-person

---

[18] Facsim. of Lérida, 1495 (?), RAE (Madrid, 1954). See also the modern edition in Barbara Matulka, *The Novels of Juan de Flores and their European Diffussion* (New York, 1931), pp. 331-370.

[19] Facsim. of Lérida 1495 (?) RAE (Madrid, 1954; Matulka, *op. cit.,* pp. 371-432.

[20] For example, the influence of the «Llanto de su madre de Leriano» in the *Cárcel de Amor* on Pleberio's lament was first discussed by Menéndez y Pelayo («La Celestina» in *Orígenes de la novela,* Edición Nacional XV, Madrid, 1943, III. 351-352). María Rosa Lida de Malkiel, among others, discusses at length the sentimental novel's antecedents for Calisto and Melibea (*Originalidad,* pp. 386-394; 445-455). Rojas himself owned a copy of the *Cárcel* (F. del Valle Lersundi, «Testamento de Fernando de Rojas», *RFE* XVI, 1929, 381-388). J. M. Aguirre (*Calisto y Melibea, amantes cortesanos,* Zaragoza, 1962) and Otis Green (*Spain and the Western Tradition,* Madison, 1963, I. 72-122) both consider *La Celestina's* relationship with «courtly love» and the sentimental romance to be of a serious and moral nature. In my opinion, the work's complexity extends beyond any possibility of classifying it as a simple *reprobatio amoris.*

dialogue situation bypassed any sort of third-person corrective. But *La Celestina* does in fact face this crisis of the third person, and faces it through Rojas' use of memory. Thibaudet's contrast of the use of time and memory in novel and drama can clarify this point:

> La vérité est que le mot de composition a un sens très diffé-rent quand il s'agit du théâtre et du roman. La composition dra-matique est fondée sur des simultanéités... On peut l'appeler une composition dans l'espace autant et plus qu'une compo-sition dans le temps... Mais le grand roman, le roman-nature, pour reprendre l'expression de tout à l'heure, ce n'est pas cela, c'est de la vie, je veux dire quelque chose qui change et quelque chose qui dure. Le vrai roman n'est pas composé... il est déposé, déposé à la façon d'une durée vécue qui se gonfle et d'une mémoire qui se forme. [21]

Rojas' characters are built upon the foundation of memory; for them time is even more of an obsession than space. This is not to say that *La Celestina* is more «novel» than «drama»; obviously it is neither. [22] Rojas' experiments with memory in *La Celestina* will lay the groundwork for memory in the *Lazarillo*, and foreshadow memory in the novel. Far from shunning the crisis of the third person, Rojas introduces into the minds of his characters a kind of memory which will not only give them a third-dimensional quality, but will provide a corrective to the dialogic situation, supplying the objective descriptions which would logically seem to be lacking in *La Ce-lestina*.

But these «objective descriptions» will in turn be colored by the relativism inherent in the human situation: memory must reflect personality. Rojas becomes the first Spanish author to attempt through memory to bridge the gap between the subjective and objective worlds of his characters. For the Spanish sentimental novelists, the past tended to be a series of external «facts», to be recounted briefly or not at all. Rojas' intuition is to see the past as memory, an essential part of human reality. But before we

---

[21] Albert Thibaudet, *Réflexions sur le roman* (Paris, 1938), p. 159.

[22] The popular classification of the work as «novela dramática» has been dis-credited by most critics. See, for example, María Rosa Lida de Malkiel, *Origina-lidad*, pp. 50-73; Gilman, *Art*, pp. 194-206; Bataillon, *La Célestine*, pp. 77ff. How-ever, for an eloquent defense of «The Dramatic Novel», see Edwin Muir, *The Struc-ture of the Novel* (London, 1928), pp. 41-61.

examine Rojas' approach to characterization, it is necessary to examine the prototype — the primitive author's development of memory as a vital concept with its own distinct literary style.

C. THE PRIMITIVE AUTHOR AND MEMORY

Even before Rojas takes up the dialogue, the primitive author begins to conceive of his characters as creatures of experienced time, figures with a past as well as voices in the present. By the end of Act I memory has evolved from its purely formal function as the vehicle for literary conventions and topics. Not surprisingly, therefore, the first clear utilization of memory in *La Celestina,* Calisto's description of Melibea, is a static and traditional vision based entirely on the medieval canon of beauty. Here Calisto's mind depends on the «commonplace book» described by Hardin Craig, [23] and even when Calisto inserts a personal note in his traditional description («Aquella proporción, que veer yo no pude, no sin duda por el bulto de fuera juzgo incomparablemente ser mejor que la que Paris juzgó entre las tres Deesas», I, 56) the author has in mind his main source, the Spanish translation of Guido de Columna's description of Helen of Troy in the *Crónica troyana,* [24] often attributed to Pero López

---

[23] «The Shackling of Accidents: A Study of Elizabethan Tragedy», *PQ* XIX (1940), 1-19.

[24] Otis Green *(HR* XIV, 1946, 254-256) explains the obvious relation of the portrait of Melibea to the commonplace medieval description of beauty. Stephen Gilman has, however, suggested to me a more exact source for this description in the *Crónica troyana* (Pamplona: Arnalt Guillén de Brocar, 1500 (?), fol. xxxviii r. & v.) Below I compare all of the *Celestina* text with selections from the longer text, the description of Helen of Troy, italicizing those passages which are identical or show marked similarities.

Comienço por los *cabellos.* ¿Vees tú las *madexas del oro* delgado, que hilan en Arabia? Más lindos son e no *resplandescen* menos. Su *longura* hasta el postrero assiento de sus pies; después crinados e atados con la delgada cuerda, como ella se los pone, no ha más menester para conuertir los hombres en piedras. (I. 54.)	Marauíllase primeramente y deléytase en contemplar el grand *resplandor* de sus *cabellos* que verdaderamente parecían *madexas de oro* y eran partidos en dos ygualdades fecha por medio dela cabeça vna pequeña cerda que los departía la qual de nieue parascía [sic] ser. Y los cabellos se tendían de cada parte en grand *longura* y copia debaxo delos quales tenía la espaciosa fruente blanca y resplandeciente amodo de vn fino cristal...
Los *ojos* verdes, rasgados; las pestanas luengas; las *cejas* delgadas e alçadas; la *nariz mediana;* la *boca pequeña;* los *dien-*	Marauíllase otrosí y deléytase en contemplar las tanbien obradas *sobrecejas* que parescían ser grand sotileza fecha por

12

de Ayala. In Act IX, Rojas will employ Elicia and Areúsa to savage this portrait of Melibea in retrospect, a modification resulting from the perspectivism which Rojas discovers in memory. [25]

---

tes *menudos* e blancos; los *labrios colora-dos* e grosezuelos; el torno del *rostro* poco más luengo que redondo; el *pecho alto; la redondeza e forma de las peque-ñas tetas,* ¿quién te la podría figurar? ¡Que se despereza el hombre cuando las mira! La tez lisa, lustrosa; el cuero suyo escurece la *nieue;* la color *mezclada,* qual ella la escogió para sí. (I. 55.)

mano a maña de los leuantados arcos tendidos por la espaciosa fruente las qua-les no eran muy pobladas de cabellos an-tes eran tan *delgadas* en parescer que re-presentauan dos filos puestos en arco... Marauíllase pues dela apostura y gracio-so parescer y vista de *sus ojos* amodo de dos resplandecientes estrellas...

Marauilláuase eso mesmo dela grand fer-mosura de su afilado *nariz. No grande ni pequeña* mas tan bien compasada que parescía ser fecha por regla y por com-pás... Y sus maxillas parescían ser rosas de viuo color. La qual por ninguna varia-ción ni mudamiento de tiempo jamás de su *rostro* no se partió *entre mesclado* vn poco de *color de nieue.* Entre las maxillas y los labros consiguiente se presentaua su *pequeña boca* y graciosa cuyos *labros* del-gados quanto cumplían eran *colorados* que parescían de color dela resplandesciente alboreda antes del salir en su viuo res-plandor... Y mas parescía en graciosidad que a todos quantos los mirauan convi-dauan a besar su guarda y cobertura delos quales tenían los *menudos dientes* que parescían ser de fino marfil...

Las *manos* pequeñas en mediana ma-nera, de dulce carne acompañadas; los *dedos luengos;* las *vñas* en ellos largas e coloradas, que parescen rubíes entre per-las. *Aquella proporción, que veer no pude, no sin duda por el bulto de fuera, juzgo incomparablemente ser mejor,* que la que París juzgó entre las tres Deesas. (I. 56.)

E sus *manos* no eran punto villanas ni gruesas, cuyos *dedos* eran *luengos* y del-gados, y las *vñas* que parescían ser de marfil. Los quales braços, manos y dedos parescían ser de color de nieue. Marauílla-se otrosí y deléytase en contemplar el su blanco y *espacioso pecho* en que eran dos *pequeñas tetillas* amodo de dos man-çanas y agudas que parescían romper sus vestiduras. Y que natura avía allí en su pecho obrados dos pequeñas *pelotas. Des-pués consideraua con mucha ymaginación todas las otras faciones y derecha estatura y cuerpo de elena por la cual él concibe y piensa enlas otras faciones y compos-turas de Elena.*

---

[25] «Fernando de Rojas ha iniciado la técnica del perspectivismo literario, ya notada desde hace mucho en Cervantes. Sus figuras humanas saben unas de otras, se representan unas a otras en varias formas; no se afectan unas a otras sólo por

It is with the appearance of the young manservant Pármeno that the primitive author first begins to develop the potential of memory in his characters. Pármeno's two expressed memories of Celestina, indoors and out, mingle literary commonplace and personal memory. The *puta vieja* passage combines a possible literary model (Petrarch)[26] and creative imagination, while Pármeno's description of Celestina in her milieu as *alcahueta* injects personal memory into an extremely recent and much less venerable literary model, Reynosa's *Coplas de las comadres*.[27] The second of Pármeno's two memories offers experiences perhaps ten years prior to the beginning of the work, and outside the time span of the dialogue.

Significantly, the *puta vieja* passage introduces stylistic elements which will reoccur in later memory passages. The reader (or listener) is suddenly confronted with an objective panorama of people, places, animals, objects, more people — «mugeres ... conbites ... fiestas ... bodas ... perros ... ganados ... ranas ... herreros ... martillos ... carpinteros e armeros, herradores, caldereros, arcadores ... labradores ... tableros ...» (I. 68-69). This perpetual-motion world is given order only by Celestina, the object of homage for the noisy crew. «Todas cosas que son hazen, a do quiera que ella está, el tal nombre representan... ¿Qué quieres más, sino que, si vna piedra topa con otra, luego suena puta vieja?» (p. 69). With this passage an objective reality in the third person —Celestina as she is known to all— begins to emerge from a fusion of memory, imagina-

---

lo que hacen sino *a través de* cómo son vividas por las otras; están relativizadas, es decir, humanizadas... Los modelos de la bella perfección —Iseo, Beatriz, Laura, Oriana, la Bella en misa, Griselda, Tristán, Amadís y sus afines— son despojados en el artístico taller de Rojas de su lejana e inalterable realidad...» Américo Castro, *La Celestina como contienda literaria* (Madrid, 1965), pp. 150-151.

[26] The Petrarchan source of this passage has been hotly disputed. Gilman first pointed out the similarity between this passage and the «unpleasant noises» passage of *De Remediis*, Preface, Book II (*Art,* pp. 169, 247), in an attempt to establish the presence of Rojas' hand in the first act (or at least to rule out «the absence of Petrarch» as a major consideration in the authorship dispute). A. D. Deyermond (*The Petrarchan Sources,* pp. 63-66) has rejected the relationship between these two passages. He ascribes the coincidences of noises to a function of «common rhetorical tradition», points out that the noises have no purpose in Petrarch, and notes that only a third of the Petrarchan noises are used.

[27] See the two articles on this topic, G. D. Trotter's «The 'Coplas de las comadres' of Rodrigo de Reynosa and 'La Celestina'» in *Homenaje a Dámaso Alonso* III (Madrid, 1963), 527-537, and Stephen Gilman and Michael Ruggerio, «Rodrigo de Reinosa and *La Celestina*», *RF* LXXIII (1961), 255-284.

tion, and literary tradition. Here, too, we may note that in this world composed of present dialogue, only the memory passages contain the imaginary speech reminiscent of the Arcipreste de Talavera's *Corbacho*. [28] «Si passa por los perros, aquello suena su ladrido: si está cerca las aues, otra cosa no cantan; si cerca los ganados, balando lo pregonan; si cerca las bestias, rebuznando dizen: ¡puta vieja!» (p. 68). The cry *puta vieja* cannot be ascribed to any specific point in time; it is an imagined statement which can occur in both the past and the future, because this «memory» is in fact a representation of Celestina as she is, was, and will be. It is through memory that an objective reality begins to emerge in the dialogue of *La Celestina.*

If Pármeno's first description of Celestina depends on literary precedent and imagination, the second description (I. 69-86) combines these two ingredients with personal experience. [29] Pármeno becomes a part of the constant and characteristic «ir y venir», the comings and goings of Celestina: «Señor, yua a la plaça e trayale de comer e acompañáuala; suplía en aquellos menesteres que mi tierna fuerça bastaua. Pero de aquel poco tiempo que la seruí, recogía la nueua memoria lo que la vejez [vieja] [30] no ha podido quitar» (I. 69-70). Memory is for the first time mentioned by name and defined as a mental function.

In recalling Celestina's profession, Pármeno introduces a first attempt at objective physical description within memory although this too draws upon Reynosa [31] — «Tiene esta buena dueña al cabo de la ciudad, allá cerca de las tenerías, en la cuesta del río, vna casa apartada, medio cayda, poco compuesta e menos abastada» (I. 70). The description, it should be noted, is somewhat abstract, for it uses vague adjectives and defines through quantity rather than through external quality — «medio ... poco ... menos». This tendency to make visions general rather than particular in the me-

---

[28] For a discussion of Alfonso Martínez de Toledo's ambivalent dialogue and monologue, see Dámaso Alonso's «El arcipreste de Talavera a medio camino entre moralista y novelista», in *De los siglos oscuros al de oro* (Madrid, 1958), pp. 125-136.

[29] The main source of this enumeration is of course, Reynosa's «Coplas de las comadres» (Gilman and Ruggerio, 268-279).

[30] «Vieja» is found in all the later editions (Zaragoza, 1507, Valencia, 1514, Seville, «1502»), «vejez» in Burgos, 1499, Toledo, 1500, Seville, 1501. I prefer the corrected version.

[31] «Allá cerca de los muros / casi en cabo dela villa / cosas haz de marauilla / vna vieja con conjuros» (Gilman and Ruggerio, 264-265).

mory passages is reinforced by the use of the imperfect tense, a stylistic trait found in most of these passages. In consequence the impression is that of persons and objects coming and going, with Celestina again as the ordering factor — «Era el primer oficio cobertura de los otros, so color del qual muchas moças destas siruientes entrauan en su casa a labrarse e a labrar camisas e gorgueras e otras muchas cosas. Ninguna venía sin torrezno, trigo, harina o jarro de vino e de las otras prouisiones que podían a sus amas furtar» (I. 70). The imperfect is used to describe Celestina moving in her surroundings, Celestina's duration in a time continuum. Only in the case of a specific act will the preterit tense be used; while the imperfect serves to stress activity around Celestina. [32]

Even when Pármeno's personal reminiscences degenerate into the ready-made and commonplace catalogue of Celestina's laboratory, this mountain of fragmented reality is all related personally to Celestina. She is the vital impulse connecting objects and the faceless people of memory. Yet the rememberer himself, Pármeno, is not lost in this panorama; he silently observes within the memory: «Muchas encubiertas vi entrar en su casa» (I. 71). The preterit tense is used; the memory of himself observing is specific.

In spite of the vague background and generalized situations in this memory passage, the primitive author has developed certain methods of giving the memory scenes a sense of immediacy. The most important of these is dialogue within the memory — «Las vnas ¡madre acá! ; las otras: ¡madre acullá! ; ¡cata la vieja! ; ¡ya viene el ama! de todos [*Trag.:* todas] muy conocida» (I. 71). This dialogue within memory will be a favorite technique of Rojas. In fact, we may regard Pármeno's initial reminiscences as our introduction to the literary style of memory passages elsewhere in the work. In future reminiscences, the concrete, objective point of reference will be the central actor of the memory (usually, Celestina), occasionally

---

[32] Gilman has expanded the grammatical interpretation of the imperfect tense in his article «The Imperfect Tense in the *Poema del Cid*», *CL,* VIII (1956), 291-306, following Damourette and Pichon's analysis of the imperfect as «the expression of conscious life progressing in time — but apart from the immediate now.» In his *Indice verbal de la Celestina,* M. Criado de Val gives a more conventional interpretation of the imperfect — «Como el lenguaje actual el imperfecto interviene para proporcionar a la narración de hechos pasados un carácter descriptivo. Su valor temporal, dentro de esta finalidad, atiende a una amplia e imprecisa zona del pasado en la que no es sistemática la separación entre pasado próximo o remoto» (*RFE* Anejo LXIV, Madrid, 1955, 106-107).

performing a specific action in the preterit tense, but usually acting «generally» in the imperfect tense. The milieu in which the actor operates is fragmentary and consists of actions, objects and dialogue which do not relate to a specific occurrence in the past, but are rather a sampling of a past reality which existed over a long period of time. In other words, past activities described are continual rather than specific.

Up to this point in the first act, the presentation of memory has been a solo performance. Towards the end of the act we get our first duet of memory, between Pármeno and Celestina, and it is here that the primitive author begins to explore memory as a way of revealing character (a technique which will be discussed in the next chapter). Previous to the encounter of Pármeno and Celestina, Pármeno has tried to «use» memory to influence another person —Calisto— although his intention was often submerged by literary cataloguing of traditional details. But the primitive author, perhaps unknowingly, has in fact begun to develop personal memory from the bare bones of literary convention, and to examine the quality of human memory (and forgetfulness) as a subjective experience. As a concomitant these memory passages become, in a sense, a substitute for third-person narration, a correction to the dialogic situation of *La Celestina*. They supply an objective reality for the characters (particularly Celestina), who otherwise tend to be subjective voices. The author's style still leans heavily on literary antecedents like the *Corbacho*. But the tense of memory —the imperfect— has been formulated. The generalized «ir y venir» of persons and objects in memory has been established, together with the concrete quality of the central characters, their duration in the imperfect, and their specific actions in the preterit, ordering the fragmented world around them.

Thus in establishing a style for the memory passages, the primitive author is setting a precedent of major innovation for Rojas. The primitive author seems instinctively to reject the classical technique of memory, as set out by the *Ad Herennium* — «the classical mnemonic based on *loci* and *imagines:* imaginary places remembered in the mind... through which the contents of memory are ordered, or built up in imaginary buildings.» [33] The main rememberers of *La Ce-*

---

[33] Frances Yates, «The Ciceronian Art of Memory» in *Medioevo e Rinascimento. Studi in onore di Bruno Nardi,* II (Florence, 1955), 874.

lestina do indeed describe a person (or image) in terms of habitual backdrops (or places). But the fixed architectural order, the attention to exact detail, has been abandoned by the primitive author: we get, instead, vague moving scenes of unspecified surroundings. With the advent of Rojas, even the enumeration of objects will largely be rejected. For Rojas, memory is not an artificial act of will, but a natural and inescapable process of the human mind.

II. MEMORY AND CHARACTER IN THE COMEDIA

With the dialogue between Pármeno and Celestina at the end of Act I,[1] the primitive author of *La Celestina* initiates the technique of the manipulation of memory by the various characters for their own purposes. But the lengthy exchange between Celestina and Pármeno is more than an illustration of self-interest acting on memory, for the primitive author is equally concerned with the different qualities of the memories displayed by his characters. Here it is important to note that Celestina herself plays a key rôle from the start: she will be the focus of the varied attitudes towards memory, the point toward which these attitudes are directed and the point at which these attitudes mingle, reform, or interfere to produce new patterns. Throughout the work both the primitive author and Rojas stress the extent of this entanglement of Celestina in the past of the other characters. Of Pármeno, she says, «Aquí está Celestina, que le vido nascer e le ayudó a criar. Su madre e yo, vña e carne» (I. 134, Act III). «Mira a Sempronio. Yo le fize hombre, de Dios en ayuso» (I. 233, Act VII). To Elicia, «Hazíalo yo mejor, quando tu abuela, que Dios aya, me mostraua este oficio: que a cabo de vn año, sabía más que ella» (I. 262, Act VII). For Areúsa, she is «Quien [*primitive eds.:* que] nunca da passo, que no piense en tu prouecho; quien tiene más memoria de ti, que de sí mesma...» (I. 247, Act VII). In addition she is entangled in the lives of the upper classes. Thus, Calisto: «Podrá ser, señora, de veynte e tres años: que aquí está Celestina, que le vido nascer e le tomó a los pies de su madre» (I. 186, Act IV). And of Pleberio's family, she claims, «Quatro años fueron mis vezinas. Tractaua con ellas, hablaua e reya de día e de noche. Mejor me conosce su ma-

---

[1] See p. 20 ff.

dre, que a sus mismas manos; avnque Melibea se ha fecho grande, muger discreta, gentil» (I. 226, Act VI). Celestina's claims may in some cases be exaggerated, yet she is in effect consolidating her influence on the lives of the other characters through her manipulation of memory. [2] It is this technique which we must now trace throughout the work by the convenient device of examining each character's own use of memory and the relationship, through and within memory, with Celestina.

A. CELESTINA AND PÁRMENO

Pármeno's youthful memories come into conflict with Celestina toward the end of Act I, where the acuteness of his juvenile memory is contrasted with her senescent forgetfulness. [3] Earlier in the act, Calisto has introduced the theme of forgetfulness («Yo temo e el temor reduze la memoria e a la prouidencia despierta», I. 87), and Pármeno remarks «ella no me conoçe, por lo poco que la seruí e por la mudança que la edad ha hecho» (I. 69). Thus the primitive author, in returning to the same theme, is emphasizing the extent to which Celestina's memory is failing. Pármeno addresses Celestina with the very words from his first memory of her:

> PÁRMENO: ¡Mas, desta flaca puta vieja!
> CELESTINA: ¡Putos días biuas, vellaquillo! e ¡cómo te atre-
> ues...!

---

[2] Menéndez y Pelayo recognized this sinister influence with the now celebrated phrases: «En lo que pudiéramos llamar *infierno estético,* entre los tipos de absoluta perversidad que el arte ha creado, no hay ninguno que iguale al de Celestina, ni siquiera el de Yago. Ambos profesan y practican la ciencia del mal por el mal; ambos dominan con su siniestro prestigio a cuantos les rodean, y los convierten en instrumentos dóciles de sus abominables tramas» («La Celestina», 357).

[3] This exchange has been one of the most discussed of the entire work. Ramiro de Maeztu noted that Celestina's arguments are based on «saber» and «hedonismo» in *Don Quijote, Don Juan y la Celestina* (Madrid, 1926), and found that her main motivation was greed (pp. 233-245; 218-232; 261-274). Under the topic «estrategia en acción», María Rosa Lida de Malkiel analyses Celestina's subtle changes of argument and incitation in this attempt to seduce Pármeno (*Originalidad,* pp. 528-529). Gilman based his concept of the internal structure of the acts (that each act is organized vitally around a central character and that character's reactions to outside influences) on the example of Pármeno's seduction (*Art,* pp. 64-74). Bataillon analyses Pármeno's description and mockery of Celestina's magic as a build-up for his corruption, and notes that in this scene Celestina's «diablerie est tout humaine, terriblement humaine» (*Célestine,* p. 67).

PÁRMENO: ¡Como te conozco...!
CELESTINA: ¿Quién eres tú?
PÁRMENO: ¿Quién? Pármeno, hijo de Alberto tu compadre, que estuue contigo vn mes [*Trag.*: un poco tiempo] que te me dio mi madre, quando morauas a la cuesta del río, cerca de las tenerías.
CELESTINA: ¡Jesú, Jesú, Jesú! ¿E tú eres Pármeno, hijo de la Claudina? (I. 98).

Far from answering the «puta vieja» epithet «con alegre cara», Celestina embarks upon the persistent, abrasive badgering which will finally become unbearable to Pármeno: «¡Pues fuego malo te queme, que tan puta vieja era tu madre como yo!» (I. 98). The battle lines are drawn; Pármeno is immediately placed on the defensive by Celestina, who will later force his capitulation. Pármeno, who has produced his credentials for Calisto («Aunque soy moço, cosas he visto asaz e el seso e la vista de las muchas cosas demuestran la experiencia», I. 89), will come off second-best in a battle with the champion manipulator of memory, Celestina. She first attempts to invite Pármeno's complicity by recalling their past together, but instead she manages to provoke his most surly reaction:

CELESTINA: ...¿Acuérdaste, quando dormías a mis pies, loquito?
PÁRMENO: Sí, en buena fe. E algunas vezes, avnque era niño, me subías a la cabeçera e me apretauas contigo e porque olías a vieja, me fuya de ti (I. 98, 99).

The ability of aged memory to whitewash and idealize the past is here defeated by the realism of the «nueva memoria».

Real memory having failed, Celestina moves on to falsified memory, invention in the past. She claims that Pármeno's father, on his deathbed, «Embió por mí e en su secreto te me encargó e me dixo sin otro testigo, sino aquél que es testigo de todas las obras e pensamientos e los coraçones e entrañas escudriña, al qual puso entre él e mí, que te buscasse e llegasse e abrigasse e, quando de complida edad fueses, tal que en tu viuir supieses tener manera e forma, te descubriesse adónde dexó encerrada tal copia de oro e plata, que basta más que la renta de tu amo Calisto» (I. 99-100). She even attempts to gloss over her earlier lapse of memory («que ha plazido a aquél... que te hallase aquí, donde solos ha tres días que sé que

moras», I. 100). Companionship and greed — these are Celestina's own motives, and she attempts to awaken these same motives in Pármeno by her artful manipulation of memory. But when this ruse fails to interest («e tengo por onesta cosa la pobreza alegre», I. 103), she falls back on the first and last of her weapons, sex («Mal sosegadilla deues tener la punta de la barriga», I. 95). The anonymous author having shown Celestina manipulating real memory (friendship) and false memory (the treasure), now moves on to the imagination. Celestina's discourse on «deleyte», again aimed at Pármeno, exploits general memory and knowledge of human nature, which she converts into imaginative action. [4] Celestina plays the male part in a brief dialogue dramatization of an imaginary love affair:

> ...esto hize, esto otro me dixo, tal donayre passamos, de tal manera la tomé, assí la besé, assí me mordió, assí la abracé, assí se allegó. ¡O qué fabla! ¡o qué gracia! ¡o qué juegos! ¡o qué besos! Vamos allá, boluamos acá, ande la música, pintemos los motes, cantemos canciones, inuenciones, justemos, qué cimera sacaremos o qué letra. Y va a la missa, mañana saldrá, rondemos su calle, mira su carta, vamos de noche, tenme el escala, aguarda a la puerta. ¿Cómo te fue? Cata el cornudo: sola la dexa. Dale otra buelta, tornemos allá (I. 107-108).

The imperfect tense is deleted in this panorama of imaginary dialogue. The verb forms begin in the preterit, advance to the present, and end in the future. In the same way, memory and imagination tend, as the work progresses, to serve as a foreshadowing of the future throughout *La Celestina*. Just as the «puta vieja» passage presaged Pármeno's words to Celestina, «Mas, desta flaca puta vieja», this passage suggests Calisto's future meetings with Melibea.

In the subsequent acts, Pármeno reinforces his role as the exponent of the defensive memory — memory as a guard against the future. Rojas articulates this attitude of Pármeno's in Act II, when the servant expounds his cause and effect theory to Calisto:

> Señor, porque perderse el otro día el neblí fue causa de tu entrada en la huerta de Melibea a le buscar, la entrada causa de la ver e hablar, la habla engendró amor, el amor parió tu pena,

---

[4] María Rosa Lida de Malkiel does not discriminate between memory and imagination, attributing to Celestina «una imaginación desinteresada, poética, evocadora del pasado o del futuro» (*Originalidad,* p. 323).

la pena causará perder tu cuerpo e el alma e hazienda. E lo que
más dello siento es venir a manos de aquella trotaconuentos, después de tres vezes emplumada (I. 121).

The past is seen as a form of fate converging on the present and impelling an unhappy future; verb tenses, progressing from preterit to
future, correspond to this vision.

Pármeno's real opportunity to exercise this new-found skill as
the exponent of defensive memories comes when the duel of memories between himself and Celestina is refought by Rojas in Act VII. [5]
Rojas has more than grasped the memory technique of the primitive
author. The latter was able to show Celestina's skill in manipulating memory and Pármeno's attempts to reply with the same weapon;
Rojas, however, will transform this game of hide-and-seek into an
acidulous match of savagery, in which the more vulnerable Pármeno
must inevitably come off second best, finally capitulating to Celestina's promise of Areúsa («Agora doy por bienempleado el tiempo
que siendo niño te seruí, pues tanto fruto trae para la mayor edad»,
I. 237). Pármeno, as always, recognizes the interrelationship and
causality in past and present events.

Once Celestina has Pármeno at her mercy, she wields memory
even more savagely, regaling him with stories of his mother's super-
ior witchcraft, emphasizing Pármeno's shame for a past which he
had tried to reject — for example, with his description to Calisto,
«mi madre, muger pobre» (I. 69, Act I). In this portrait of Pármeno's mother, Celestina even succeeds in mastering the negative
vision of the past. She converts it into a positive vision, and in-
fuses it with a certain nostalgia and macabre charm:

> ¿Quién era todo mi bien e descanso, sino tu madre, más que
> mi hermana e comadre? ¡O qué graciosa era! ¡O qué desem-
> buelta, limpia, varonil! Tan sin pena ni temor se andaua a me-
> dia noche de cimenterio en cimenterio, buscando aparejos para
> nuestro oficio, como de día. Ni dexava christianos ni moros ni
> judíos, cuyos enterramientos no visitaua. De día los acechaua, de
> noche los desenterraua (I. 238, Act. VII).

Here Rojas explores a possibility which the primitive author had
ignored — the aged crone does have a weakness for her former gran-

---

[5] Gilman emphasizes the importance of this parallelism in the acts (*Art*,
p. 118).

deur and for the companionship afforded by earlier years. Although Rojas is using the same stylistic technique developed by the unknown author, the feeling of this passage is immediate. Celestina includes specific reminiscences in the general panorama of the past — «Siete dientes quitó a vn ahorcado con vnas tenazicas de pelarcejas, mientra yo le descalcé los çapatos» (I. 239). These observations are wasted on Pármeno («No la medre Dios más a esta vieja», I. 240), who retaliates by entering upon an exchange of unpleasantries with a most savage attack. «Dime, señora, quando la justicia te mandó prender, estando yo en tu casa, ¿teníades mucho conocimiento?» (I. 241). Celestina is taken aback and echoes a notion that everything is forgotten, an idea usually found in Sempronio's mouth, but which once again proves that Celestina can beat anyone at the game of manipulating memory: «...juntas nos dieron la pena essa vez... Pero muy pequeño eres tú. Yo me espanto cómo te acuerdas, que es la cosa que más oluidada está en la cibdad. Cosas son que pasan por el mundo» (I. 242). But Pármeno will not let her off the hook so easily: «Verdad es; pero del pecado lo peor es la perseuerancia» (I. 242). Celestina turns on him; «Pues espera, que yo te tocaré donde te duela... prendieron quatro veces a tu madre, que Dios aya, sola» (I. 242). Then follows the description of the persecution of Claudina — «E avn la vna le leuantaron que era bruxa, porque la hallaron de noche con vnas candelillas, cogiendo tierra de vna encruzijada, e la touieron medio día en vna escalera en la plaça puesta, vno como rocadero pintado en la cabeça» (I. 243). But the altercation finally dies down, because Pármeno must not be alienated again. Celestina briefly renews the fabrication of the treasure, but Pármeno decides to set aside the past for good — «hablemos en los presentes negocios, que nos va más que en traer los passados a la memoria. Bien se te acordará, no ha mucho que me prometiste que me harías hauer a Areúsa...» (I. 245). With these words Pármeno introduces the theme of the importance of memory to Celestina's profession, and she swiftly replies «Si te lo prometí, no lo he oluidado ni creas que he perdido con los años la memoria» (I. 246).

With the reintroduction of the conflict between aged and young memory, the duel between Pármeno and Celestina comes to an end. Pármeno's truthful memories have been defeated by Celestina's experience, for in order to prevail, the unexpurgated reporting of a fresh memory needs a stronger vessel than Pármeno, vulnerable through his shame and appetites. Celestina's memory, although patchy and inclined to sentimental idealization, is still sufficiently experienced and crafty to bring to bear the whole range of destructive possibilities, both of appealing to Pármeno through past reminiscence, and of punishing him for his «treachery». From this point forward, Pármeno abandons his own fears of causality and his fatalism, and like Sempronio, he will ignore the lessons of the past. After his encounter with Areúsa, he copies the behavior which he has criticized in the forgetful and oblivious lover, Calisto.

B. CELESTINA AND SEMPRONIO

The real antagonist of memory, however, is not Pármeno but Sempronio. Although he and Celestina engage only once in an actual clash over the merits of memory, the contrast between the *alcahueta* and the manservant is implied throughout the work. In Act II, when Rojas first takes over the dialogue, Sempronio remarks «que fiar en lo temporal e buscar materia de tristeza, que es ygual género de locura... En el contemplar ésta es la pena de amor, en el oluidar el descanso» (I. 117-118). Typically, Rojas' sense of irony manipulates his characters, for Sempronio unrealistically expects forgetfulness to isolate the human being from the possibly harmful consequences of interaction. However, he will pretend to use memory in order to invent past courage and to justify cowardice, and this will lead to his death. Pármeno, on the other hand, sees the inevitable consequences of the past in the present, and still hopes that the fatal process can be halted. But he fails to take his own advice, and rage at being reminded of his mother's past leads to his death as well.

In Act III, Sempronio articulates his temporal theory at length. Again forgetfulness is lauded as the only possible escape from adverse fortune:

> Que no ay cosa tan difícile de çofrir en sus principios, que el tiempo no la ablande e faga comportable... El mal e el bien, la prosperidad e aduersidad, la gloria e pena, todo pierde con el tiempo la fuerça de su acelerado principio... Cada día vemos nouedades e las oyemos e las passamos e dexamos atrás. Diminúyelas el tiempo, házelas contingibles... Todo es assí, todo passa desta manera, todo se oluida, todo queda atrás... Que la costum-

bre luenga amansa los dolores, afloxa e deshaze los deleytes, desmengua las marauillas. Procuremos prouecho, mientra pendiere la contienda (I. 129-132). [6]

Elicia's sloughing off of her mourning in the «Tractado de Centurio» will be an ironic example of Sempronio's philosophy. Not only is oblivion an escape, it is an inevitable process.

Shortly after Sempronio discusses the disappearance of the past in forgetfulness, Celestina's recollection of Claudina is placed in direct opposition to the manservant's philosophy. Rojas shows at length that memory for her can be a reconstruction of friendship and social experience, a memory of the time when real communion with another person was possible — «Juntas comíamos, juntas dormíamos, juntas auíamos nuestros solazes, nuestros plazeres, nuestros consejos e conciertos» (I. 134, Act III). [7] For Sempronio, time is an ally; for the ancient Celestina it is the enemy — « ¡O muerte muerte! A quántos priuas de agradable compañía! » (I. 135).

The literary technique employed by Rojas in this passage is similar to the «memory» style evolved in the first act; Claudina is seen in her habitual offices, acting in the imperfect in a generalized, objective world. [8] The difference is that she is accompanied by Celestina — «Si yuamos por la calle, donde quiera que ouiessemos sed, entráuamos en la primera tauerna y luego mandaua echar medio açum-

---

[6] Gilman remarks of Sempronio's theories (Art, p. 135) that «their cynicism is in fundamental accord with the corrosive nature of Sempronio's understanding of time. Sempronio is perversely delighted with temporality rather than sadder and wiser, and he concludes not with 'menosprecio del mundo' but with 'menosprecio de la persona', that very same 'persona' whose life is thematically subject to dimensionality».

[7] In analysing the professional conscience of Celestina, María Rosa Lida de Malkiel remarks only that Celestina «guarda respetuosamente la memoria de sus maestras... su reverencia por Claudina» (Originalidad, p. 518). Gilman goes further than this; he notes that «the inhabitants of La Celestina cannot derive from their separate solitudes the consolations of Vaucluse. I instead they all strive frenziedly for company of one sort or another... Even the apparently self-sufficient Celestina refers again and again nostalgically to her past companionship with Claudina... Despite the vicious irony of Rojas' treatment of these aspects of Celestina's life and death, on their own terms they are genuine» («Fernando de Rojas as Author», RF LXXVI, 1964, 283).

[8] Celestina also has sentimental memories of Alberto, Claudina's husband. When she finally begins to subvert Pármeno, she exults, «Por ende gózome, Pármeno, que ayas limpiado las turbias telas de tus ojos e respondido al reconoscimiento, discreción e engenio sotil de tu padre, cuya persona, agora representada en mi memoria, enternece los ojos piadosos, por do tan abundantes lágrimas vees derramar» (I. 110, Act I).

bre para mojar la boca...» (I. 136). Here the imperfect tense operates in its 'sentimental' function — to bring the listeners or readers
into closer communion with the actors of memory.[9] Details are also
more refined in this passage than they were in the first act; external
reality is less of a mindless accumulation of objects and persons, and
corresponds to a more measured logical progression through space:
«Si yo traya el pan, ella la carne. Si yo ponía la mesa, ella los man-
teles» (I. 135). Finally, the imaginary dialogue is still present
— «que en todo el camino no oye peor de 'Señora Claudina'»
(I. 135).

In the third act memory comes under a vital analysis by two
characters, Sempronio and Celestina. Sempronio extols forgetfulness
as a device by which to evade reality; Celestina demonstrates how
memory can create an ideal which may be superimposed on reality.
These two views correspond to the life rôles of the characters — Sempronio is old enough to be totally cynical, not old enough for this
cynicism to be tempered and mellowed. Celestina, old and more
disenchanted with life, has learned the virtue of distorting the past
and of finding respite in this idealization. Rojas has begun to develop
more fully the idea of the different qualities of memory in different
ages. Celestina's memory will become typically that of an old
person — her memory of the remote past acute, her memory in the
present fuzzy at best. Sempronio displays a perfectly adequate memory of present occurrences, but has a youthful disregard for the
past; his path —he thinks— leads into the future. Pármeno's
«nueva memoria» of the distant past is as acute as Celestina's for
traumatic rather than pleasant reasons, in keeping with the memories
of a post-adolescent who has suffered an unpleasant childhood.
Thus Pármeno's negativism is an attempt to repudiate his past through
memory. Rather than forgetting his earlier life, he tries to discredit
that life and Celestina's rôle in his past by subjecting it to the harsh
and exacting light of his memories.

Celestina's reminiscences in this case seem to be directed almost
entirely within herself, for there is no good reason for her to regale
Sempronio with this discourse. Her desire in so doing is to impress
Sempronio with her prowess as a witch, yet the description of her
friendship with Claudina fulfills this function only peripherally, by
recounting her vast experience in life, and her business association

---

[9] See pp. 15-16, above.

with Pármeno's mother. In Act IX, Celestina will aim her reminiscences about the «good old days» at Lucrecia, but again she becomes so entangled within her own eloquence, that Sempronio will renew his argument and admonish her characteristically: «Madre, ningund prouecho trae la memoria del buen tiempo, si cobrar no se puede: antes tristeza» (II. 48).

But remarkably, Sempronio is the one character who best understands the full importance of memory to Celestina in her profession. [10] In an attempt to retain his ascendancy over Pármeno after his night of love in Act IX, Sempronio shows Pármeno that his memories of Celestina are much fresher than his friend's. Although the young Pármeno lived with Celestina, Sempronio has no need to fill the gap of memory with literary borrowings.

> Verdad es: pero mal conoces a Celestina. Quando ella tiene que hazer, no se acuerda de Dios ni cura de santidades. Quando hay que roer en casa, sanos están los santos; quando va a la yglesia con sus cuentas en la mano, no sobra el comer en casa. Avnque ella te crió, mejor conozco yo sus propriedades que tú. Lo que en sus cuentas reza es los virgos que tiene a cargo e quántos enamorados ay en la cibdad e quántas moças tiene encomendadas e qué despenseros [le dan ración e quál lo mejor e cómo les llaman por nombre, porque quando los encontrare no hable como estraña] [*primitive eds.*: hay en la ciudad] e qué canónigo es más moço e franco. Quando menea los labios es fengir mentiras, ordenar cautelas para hauer dinero: por aquí le entraré, esto me responderá, estotro replicaré. Assí viue ésta, que nosotros mucho honrramos (II. 25).

With this passage, Sempronio analyses brilliantly the importance of dialogue and memory and imagination to Celestina — these are the essence of her profession; «porque quando los encontrare no hable como estraña». Possible dialogue, with Celestina as the speaker, is the crux of this passage, [11] «por aquí le entraré, esto me responderá,

---

[10]   The cynical Sempronio's remarkable clarity of vision extends into his other memories. For example, he gives Pármeno a succinct description of Calisto's lover's trance (II. 16, Act VIII). «Allí está tendido en el estrado cabo (*Trag.*: cabe) la cama, donde le dexaste anoche. Que ni ha dormido ni está despierto. Si allá entro, ronca; si me salgo, canta o deuanea. No le tomo tiento, si con aquello pena o descansa.»

[11]   More usually this passage is seen as «anticlerical» (Cejador, II, 25, n. 13) or as an illustration of Celestina's peculiar type of religiosity (Lida de Malkiel, p. 511).

estotro replicaré». The passage is not so much memory as an imaginative tableau of Celestina functioning in the present and plotting in the future. It is interesting that Sempronio intentionally avoids Celestina's brand of sentimental reminiscence; the antagonist of memory finds this distasteful. «Objective reality» is once more ancillary to Celestina, who animates the surrounding world of «virgos», «moços», and «canónigos» with her dialogue and her memory.

C. Celestina and the Women of the «Comedia»

Rojas first examines the implications of memory in the characters of his women in Act IV, where Celestina again serves as a stimulus for the various attitudes of Alisa, Lucrecia and Melibea. Here character analysis is found within each woman's memory of Celestina. Lucrecia, for example, reveals herself as basically a practical and slightly cynical young woman (not so sheltered as her cousin Areúsa would think), [12] when Celestina's appearance and feeble excuse elicits the line «Marrauíllome de ti, que no es éssa tu costumbre ni sueles dar passo sin prouecho» (I. 159). Alisa, on the other hand, proves to be the sort of scatterbrain who will not only fail to recognize Lucrecia's copious description of Celestina (« ¡Jesú, señora! más conoscida es esta vieja que la ruda. No sé cómo no tienes memoria de la que empicotaron por hechizera, que vendía las moças a los abades e descasaua mill casados» I. 160), but will later leave her only daughter in Celestina's hands. [13] It is a name alone which evokes the memory, although the superstitious Lucrecia is reluctant to name aloud the scar-faced and demoniac figure of Celestina.

Melibea is the next to recognize Celestina, and her reaction points up the fact that she has reached maturity only recently. «Vieja te has parado. Bien dizen que los días no se van en balde. Assí goze de mí, no te conociera, sino por essa señaleja de la cara. Figúrasme que eras hermosa. Otra pareces, muy mudada estás» (I. 170). When Lucre-

---

[12] María Rosa Lida de Malkiel sees Lucrecia's main character traits, other than honesty, as «buen seso, poca imaginación» (*Originalidad*, pp. 643-644).

[13] As Gilman remarks, «How well Rojas arranges for Alisa to betray herself in a few short sentences as a heedless bourgeoise! »; «Rebirth of a Classic: Celestina», in *Varieties of Literary Experience,* ed. Stanley Burnshaw (New York, 1962), p. 294, revised and reprinted in Spanish in my edition of *La Celestina.* Alisa's action is also the best support for arguments that Celestina's witchcraft is, indeed, eficacious. Not surprisingly, Rojas makes the situation ambiguous — either character weakness or witchcraft can explain the scene.

cia laughs at Melibea's idealized childhood impressions, including her failure to notice Celestina's scar, and points out that only a short time has passed since they lived next door to the ugly old woman, Melibea takes umbrage and defends her memory. «No es tan poco tiempo dos años» (I. 171; omitted from *Trag.*) For the adolescent Melibea these are the two long years in which she has reached maturity, «después que a mí me sé conocer» (II. 148, Act XVI). [14] Celestina reemphasizes this recent maturity with her later remark, «Melibea se ha fecho grande, muger discreta, gentil» (I. 226, Act VI). Character is filtered through memory, and expressed by different senses of time. For Lucrecia, it was only yesterday that Celestina liver next door («Celestina madre, seas bienvenida. ¿Quál Dios te traxo por estos barrios no acostumbrados?» I. 159, Act IV). For Alisa, the past has all but disappeared and must be copiously documented. For Melibea, it seems a long time since Celestina lived near by.

As for Celestina, she again declares herself an opponent and victim of time — «Señora, ten tú el tiempo que no ande; terné yo mi forma, que no se mude» (I. 171). Once more she falsifies time and memory, strangely enough, for the sake of personal vanity — «Pero también yo encanecí temprano e parezco de doblada edad... Mira cómo no soy vieja como me juzgan» (I. 171-172). These cross-references in memory are common; Pármeno has already mentioned «Celestina con sus seys dozenas de años acuestas» (I. 126, Act II). And Celestina herself admits to seventy years.

Celestina's first personal interview with Melibea reverts to the elementary type of memory which appeared in Act I, a memory depending largely on literary convention. Her commonplace description of Calisto («en franqueza, Alexandre, en esfuerço, Etor» I. 185) [15] is of course aimed at Melibea and parallels Calisto's traditional literary vision in the first act, when he saw Melibea as a Helen of Troy. But together with this standard, and even compulsory description, Celestina introduces the personal note which continues to involve her in the past of all the major characters; «Podrá ser, señora, de veynte e tres años; que aquí está Celestina, que le vido nascer e le tomó a los pies de su madre» (I. 186). Literary convention also

---

[14] «Hace dos años —dos años decisivos de adolescencia— que Melibea no ha visto a Celestina» (Lida de Malkiel, p. 171).

[15] «Enumeración de parangones en que predomina la alusión clásica, rara vez usada por la vieja y sólo en interés...» (Lida de Malkiel, p. 525).

serves to falsify memory and to introduce a strong note of irony in Celestina's further descriptions of Calisto. His deficient musical abilities, much mocked by his servants, are compared to those of Orpheus (I. 187).

This skilful counterpoint of memory is reinforced in Act X, the «reprise» of Act IV. The power of the name in memory is admitted by Melibea after she faints when Celestina names Calisto — «Muchos e muchos días son passados que esse noble cauallero me habló en amor. Tanto me fue entonces su habla enojosa, quanto, después que tú me le tornaste a nombrar, alegre» (II. 61). These revelations gain importance in relation to the lovers' duet of memory in Act XII, and, as in the case of Pármeno, show the adolescent Melibea in her basic helplessness against the manipulator of memory.

Celestina, too, recalls her «heroic» struggle of Act IV to overcome her fear of the first visit, and Lucrecia relates the signs of love which she has noticed in Melibea. These two reminiscences gain value later when compared with parallel passages in Act XI, Celestina's account to Calisto of her visit to Melibea. This series of memories is capped by a real cross-reference to Act IV. Alisa finally realizes the potential danger of Celestina to her daughter's honor: «Sabe ésta con sus trayciones, con sus falsas mercadurías, mudar los propósitos castos. Daña la fama. A tres vezes que entra en vna casa, engendra sospecha» (II. 65, Act X). Lucrecia remarks drily, «Tarde acuerda nuestra ama». [16] In the two symmetrical scenes, the profiles of the women in Pleberio's household have been sharpened by their various types of memory. Memory (or forgetfulness) is the key to Alisa's scatterbrained character; to a lesser extent it highlights important facets of the astute Lucrecia and the adolescent Melibea.

Celestina's relationship with Elicia and Areúsa is much more intimate. Memory is one of the main links between Celestina and Elicia; on two occasions Elicia scolds Celestina for her forgetfulness. The first occasion is minor; Celestina sends Elicia for one of her articles of witchcraft in Act III and Elicia complains «Madre, no está

---

[16] María Rosa Lida de Malkiel tries to redeem Alisa somewhat, explaining this sequence as merely representative of many warnings:

«Alisa, que tanto se jacta de su crianza de la hija... la ha prevenido muchas veces, y el final del acto X no es más que una de todas esas prevenciones, soberbiamente escogida, ya que llega cuando Melibea está tan trastornada por su pasión que no tiene escrúpulo en responder a la solicitud de su madre con una odiosa mentira.» (*Originalidad*, p. 179).

donde dizes; jamás te acuerdas a cosa que guardas» (I. 145). Celestina replies «No infinjas porque está aquí Sempronio, ni te ensoberuezcas...» (I. 146). This domestic squabbling [17] is again emphasized in Act VII, when Elicia berates the aging Celestina for her loss of memory, a faculty which, as Sempronio points out in the next act, is the key to her profession. Elicia reminds Celestina of the betrothed girl who must be mended; Celestina cannot remember her in spite of a copious description, a scene which curiously recalls her antagonist Alisa's recent loss of memory. «¡O cómo caduca la memoria!» complains Elicia, but Celestina has her excuses — «No te marauilles, hija, que quien en muchas partes derrama su memoria, en ninguna la puede tener» (I. 261). Celestina, unlike the other characters of the drama, is not reminded of this case by a name, but by an *object*. «¿La de la manilla es? Ya sé por quién dizes» (I. 261). People are equated with objects in Celestina's system of values, just as the people surrounding Celestina are reduced to the inanimate and faceless level in the memory passages of the work.

In Act VII Celestina also encounters Areúsa; she characterizes herself to the girl as «Quien no te quiere mal, por cierto; quien nunca da passo, que no piense en tu prouecho; quien tiene más memoria de ti, que de sí mesma; vna enamorada tuya, avnque vieja» (I. 247). Trying to persuade Areúsa to accept Pármeno, she not only harps comically on her old theme of companionship («Vna alma sola ni canta ni llora» I. 255) but she also paints a tableau of the advantages Elicia has gleaned from their association: «¡Ay! ¡ay! hija, si viesses el saber de tu prima e qué tanto le ha aprovechado mi criança e consejos e qué gran maestra está» (I. 254).

These two disciples of Celestina will not be separated for long; in the banquet scene of Act IX they provide catty memories of Melibea which contrast with Calisto's topical portrait in the first Act, but which probably also owe a considerable amount to the medieval commonplaces of cosmetics, and the grotesque woman. [18] This memory is obviously colored by jealousy (or as Sempronio puts it, «Hermana, paréceme aquí que cada buhonero alaba sus agujas» II. 33),

---

[17] «Only Celestina and her companion, Elicia, exhibit any sort of domestic harmony (in this Rojas displays the full bite of his irony), a weird and violent harmony which is maintained cynically by both of them» (Gilman, «Rebirth of a Classic», p. 294).

[18] This discussion also could be considered one of Rojas' contributions to the fifteenth-century feminist debate.

as has been foreshadowed by Calisto's imaginative forays into the female world in Act VI — «Pues quantas oy son nascidas, que della tengan noticia, se maldizen, querellan a Dios, porque no se acordó dellas, quando a esta mi señora hizo. Consumen sus vidas, comen sus carnes con embidia, danles siempre crudos martirios, pensando con artificio ygualar con la perfición, que sin trabajo dotó a ella natura» (I. 227). But the vice of cosmetics which he attributes to others is turned against Melibea by Elicia and Areúsa:

> Todo el año se está encerrada con mudas de mill suziedades. Por vna vez que aya de salir donde puede ser vista, enuiste su cara con hiel e miel, con vnas tostadas e higos passados e con otras cosas que por reuerencia de la mesa dexo de dezir. Las riquezas las hazen a éstas hermosas e ser alabadas; que no las gracias de su cuerpo. Que assí goze de mí, vnas tetas tiene, para ser donzella, como si tres vezes houiese parido: no parecen sino dos grandes calabaças. El vientre no se le he visto; pero, juzgando por lo otro, creo que le tiene tan floxo como vieja de cincuenta años (II. 32-33).

With the arrival of Lucrecia, hostilities cease and Areúsa launches her imaginative attack on the position of a maidservant, the most patent imitation of the Arcipreste de Talavera in the work — «Ven acá, mala muger, la gallina hauada no paresce: pues búscala presto; si no, en la primera blanca de tu soldada la contaré» (II. 42). But in her defense of independence Areúsa does make one personal reminiscence which parallels Melibea's later words — «Por esto me viuo sobre mí, desde que me sé conocer» (II. 41). If Celestina and later Melibea are the champions of companionship, Areúsa pathetically advances the cause of solitude — but, as she revealed to Celestina in Act VII, in reality she is under constant surveillance by her neighbors and by Centurio. Although Elicia and Areúsa are united in their hatred of the privileged Melibea, memory sheds some light on the contrasting characters of the two girls: Elicia, dependent on the offices of Celestina, and Areúsa, the vocal yet helplessly trapped champion of solitude and independence. Areúsa's memory is active only as imagination, as a means of satirizing what she considers undesirable conditions. Her personal isolation cuts her off even from her own past.

Celestina, by contrast with the younger women she dominates, again spins the web of memory in this act in order to win over Lucrecia to their side. [19]   Celestina herself is caught up in the recreation of the good old days.   But the ploy will work; Lucrecia is duped:

> Por cierto, ya se me hauía oluidado mi principal demanda e mensaje con la memoria de esse tan alegre tiempo como has contado e assí me estuuiera vn año sin comer, escuchándote e pensando en aquella vida buena que aquellas moças gozarían, que me parece e semeja que estó yo agora en ella (II. 49).

As for the reminiscence itself, Celestina once more declares herself an enemy of time, which in her prosperous days twenty years before ordained that her fortune must rise and fall — «Yo vi, mi amor, a esta mesa, donde agora están tus primas assentadas, nueue moças de tus días, que la mayor no passaua de dieziocho años e ninguna hauía menor de quatorze» (II. 43-44).

Here Celestina's panorama of the honorable past is the most advanced, stylistically, of the memory passages, although it depends on a seemingly traditional anti-clerical satire.   Again the vision is in the imperfect tense and abstract, and people are faceless, often identified with objects — «En entrando por la yglesia, vía derrocar bonetes en mi honor, como si yo fuera vna duquesa... Vno a vno y dos a dos, venían a donde yo estaua...» (II. 45).   Indirect dialogue appears — «Vnos me llamaban señora, otros tía, otros enamorada, otros vieja honrrada» (I. 45). [20]   Celestina remembers honor and material goods;   people are transformed into faceless gift-bearers and sycophants, bringing food and wines.   The cataloguing of objects makes a brief reappearance, and the comestibles seem to move of their own accord — «E embiauan sus escuderos e moços a que me acompañassen, e apenas era llegada a mi casa, quando entrauan por mi puerta muchos pollos e gallinas, ansarones, anadones, perdizes, tórtolas, perniles de tocino, tortas de trigo, lechones» (II. 46). «Pues otros curas sin renta, no era ofrecido el bodigo, quando en besando el filigrés la estola, era del primero boleo en mi casa» (II. 47).

This hedonistic vision comes to a climax with Celestina's review

---

[19]   María Rosa Lida de Malkiel first suggested that this speech is aimed at Lucrecia, whom Celestina needs as an accomplice (*Originalidad*, p. 643).

[20]   Américo Castro points out the relation of this passage with the *Misa de amor* theme, in which the attractive young girl is the object of all eyes in the church, and concludes: «Esto no es una parodia. Las parodias existen a expensas de lo parodiado, y no per se» (*La Celestina como contienda literaria*, p. 97).

of the wines — «avnque tengo la diferencia de los gustos e sabor en la boca, no tengo la diuersidad de sus tierras en la memoria» (II. 47). The senses finally triumph over memory and reason. But Celestina suddenly returns to the present, and the activist verges on a state of philosophical despair — «No sé cómo puedo vivir, cayendo de tal estado» (II. 47). This final anguished vision of the past goes beyond mere manipulation of memory to exert influence on others; it defies even the analysis of *codicia, honra, compañía* in Celestina's hierarchy of motivation. The unspoken antagonist in this passage is not just Fortune but *olvido* — the state of being forgotten, a state of living death from which Celestina attempts to return, by recreating the past with words and trapping her listeners, particularly Lucrecia, in this creation.

D. CELESTINA AND CALISTO: THE LOSS OF MEMORY THROUGH LOVE

In the fifth and sixth acts, Celestina twice recalls her interview with Melibea, once for herself and once for Calisto. These two recollections provide the best evidence of the transformation of the past through memory, and of Celestina's talent for using the past for her own benefit. In the fifth act, Celestina recalls the interview in order to foster her self-pride and personal value. She accords herself a heroic rank in the annals of *alcahuetería:*

> ¡O rigurosos trances! ¡O cuerda osadía! ¡O gran sufrimiento! ¡E qué tan cercana estuue de la muerte, si mi mucha astucia no rigiera con el tiempo las velas de la petición! ¡O amenazas de donzella braua!... Nunca huyendo huye la muerte al couarde! ¡O quántas erraran en lo que yo he acertado! ¿Qué fizieran en tan fuerte estrecho estas nueuas maestras de mi oficio, sino responder algo a Melibea por donde se perdiera quanto yo con buen callar he ganado? (I. 193-194).

But in her account to Calisto, Celestina wisely concentrates on Melibea, and diminishes her own rôle. «E yo a todo esto arrinconada, encogida, callando, muy gozosa con su ferocidad» (I. 214, Act VI). Celestina, in fact, presents herself restraining her senses and employing her mind instead — «yo no dexaua mis pensamientos estar bagos ni ociosos» (I. 214). With the actual description of Melibea, Rojas is again writing within a literary convention of the «signs of love», though this material is exaggerated by Celestina for Calisto's benefit,[21] to impress him with her own bravery without detracting from the image of the aroused Melibea. Thus the description of Melibea in sensory terms — «mirándome», «escuchando fasta ver», «diziendo», «herida de aquella dorada frecha, que del sonido de tu nombre le tocó», «las manos enclauijadas», «acoceando con los pies el suelo duro» (I. 212-214). The preterit tense intrudes in this instance of description of a concrete occurence within the work, but the present participle dominates, lending the realistic touch of immediacy to the scene.[22]

When she describes her connections with Pleberio's family, Celestina also resorts to memory of a more remote past in order to strengthen her authority over Calisto. «Quatro años fueron mis vezinas. Tractaua con ellas, hablaua e reya de día e de noche. Mejor me conosce su madre, que a sus mismas manos; aunque Melibea se ha fecho grande, muger discreta, gentil» (I. 226). Memory provides a cross-reference to an earlier passage, the recognition scene between the women (Act IV), and the irony of Celestina's comment about Alisa is obvious since her memory of Celestina did not even reach back two years.

Calisto's replies to Celestina are consistent with his role as the courtly lover. Rojas obviously recognizes the anonymous author's source for the earlier traditional description of Melibea, because he too shows further influence of the *Crónica troyana* — «Si oy fuera viua Elena, por quien tanta muerte houo de griegos e troyanos, o la hermosa Pulicena, todas obedescerían a esta señora por quien yo peno. Si ella se hallara presente en aquel debate de la mançana con las tres diosas, nunca sobrenombre de discordia le pusieran» (I. 226-227). He continues with the comparison of other women to Melibea,[23] and offers the reader a taste of that combination of imagina-

---

[21] Lucrecia's interpolated listing of the signs of love in Act X may have been due to Rojas' sense of symmetry — one report was not enough, and Lucrecia's modest account gives perspective to Celestina's exaggerations (II. 64).

[22] A parallel scene is played in Act X, when Celestina reenacts for Melibea the prelude to their first encounter:

> Verdad es que ante que me determinasse, assí por el camino, como en tu casa, estuue en grandes dubdas si te descobriría mi petición. Visto el gran poder de tu padre, temía; mirando la gentileza de Calisto, osaua; vista tu discreción, me recelaua; mirando tu virtud e humanidad, me esforçaua. En lo vno fallaua el miedo e en lo otro la seguridad (II. 62).

Celestina gives a remarkably accurate picture of her emotions and reasoning, omitting only her motivation (greed) and her cynicism about the discretion of young ladies.

[23] See p. 33.

tion and literary reminiscence which becomes his speciality in the additional acts. For the present, however, Calisto's forte is not memory, but the traditional lover's forgetfulness. The «infirmity» of love has caused the illness of forgetfulness, [24] the implied contrast being with natural loss of memory through old age.

---

[24] Forgetfulness was actually considered a disease at this time. In the *Sumario de la medicina en romance,* Doctor Villalobos dedicated this verse to «memoria corrupta»;

> Memoria corrupta es vna enfermedad
> con quien la memoria oluida lo que era,
> y viene al celebro de alguna frialdad
> compuesta con humido o con sequedad
> de humor o sin él en la parte trasera;
> si su causa fue sequedad y calor,
> o qualquier qualidad, ya tú sabes la cura;
> pero si conosces flemático humor,
> xarab de cantueso digere mejor,
> después con cochias purgalle procura.

(*Algunas obras de Francisco López de Villalobos,* SBE 24, ed. Antonio María Fabié, Madrid, 1886, pp. 320-321). Vives, too, was examining the topic of forgetfulness in his dialogues:

MENDOZA: Quamdiu dixit?
MANRIQUE: Horas duas.
MENDOZA: Ex tam longa oratione tam paucula mandasti memoriae?
MANRIQUE: Mandavi quidem memoriae; sed ea noluit retinere.
MENDOZA: Plane dolium habes fialiarum Danai.

(«Scriptio», in *Diálogos latinos de Luis Vives,* ed. C. Fernández, Barcelona, 1940, p 76.) Finally, the topic of romantic oblivion was so popular in the fifteenth century that Erasmus managed to include it in his *Lingua:*

> Est quidem impotens affectus ira, sed magnam habet temulentian et uoluptas. Dulce est amanti sine fine garrire de suis amoribus, at non est eadem uoluptas ijs, qui uacant amore. Amantes enim ob impotentiam affectus quo tenetur no solum existimant, omnibus hominibus esse curae quod agunt, uerum etiam res inanimas perinde quasi sentiant alloquuntur: uelut apud Plautum adolescens cum pessulis et ostio litigat, sic cum lectulo uoluptatis conscio, sic cum lucernula conscia, sic cum uiolis ac strophijs et anulis ab amica missis, aut ad amicam ituris, prolixas miscent fabulas. (*Lingua per Des. Erasmum Roterodamum,* [Nuremberg] 1525, fol. 114 verso).

A contemporary Spanish rendition reads:

> Impetuosa passión es la yra: pero grande es la borrachez del deleyte. El enamorado nunca querría dexar de hablar en sus amores: los que no aman no huelgan de aquello: piensan los enamorados con la ceguera que tienen que no solamente los hombres tienen cuydado delo que hazen: pero aun hablan con las cosas insensibles: como vn enamorado de quien habla Plauto: que reñía con las aldauas y con la puerta: y desta manera hablan con la cama: con la candela que les alumbra: con las flores y anillos que le embía su amiga: o que an de yr a ella. (*La lengua de Erasmo roterodamo nueuamente romançada,/por muy elegante estilo,* n.p., 1533, fol. lxiiii.)

In the eighth act, Rojas draws an ironic parallel between the two «lovers» Pármeno and Calisto — both suffer loss of memory through love. After his night with Areúsa, Pármeno loses track of time: «¿Amanesce o qué es esto, que tanta claridad está en esta cámara?» (II. 7). When he asks Sempronio of Calisto — «¿E que nunca me ha llamado ni ha tenido memoria de mí?» Sempronio answers «No se acuerda de sí, ¿acordarse ha de ti?» (II. 17). Although Pármeno attempts to relive his night of love and extol his lady in courtly fashion with rhetorical questions («¡O hermano! ¿qué te contaría de sus gracias de aquella muger, de su habla e hermosura de cuerpo? Pero quede para más oportunidad» II. 15), he lacks the poetic imagination of Calisto. Lamely, he harks back to Celestina's evaluation of the past — «Bien me dezía la vieja que de ninguna prosperidad es buena la posesión sin compañía» (II. 9).

Sempronio, too, joins in the general declamation in Act IX. Having obviously become infatuated with Melibea, he compares himself to Calisto in a mock-courtly version of the signs of love (but attributing the cause to Elicia):

> Señora, en todo concedo con tu razón, que aquí está quien me causó algún tiempo andar fecho otro Calisto, perdido el sentido, cansado el cuerpo, la cabeça vana, los días mal dormiendo, las noches todas velando... (II. 38).

Yet in the previous act he has advised Calisto «Oluida, señor, vn poco a Melibea y verás la claridad» (II. 19).

For her part, Celestina paints an imaginative tableau of the same oblivious behavior described by Sempronio, attributing it to all lovers:

> E si alguna cosa destas la natural necessidad les fuerça a hazer, están en el acto tan oluidados que comiendo se oluida la mano de lleuar la vianda a la boca. Pues si con ellos hablan, jamás conueniente respuesta bueluen. Allí tienen los cuerpos; con sus amigas los coraçones e sentidos (II. 37).

By Act XII, a new Calisto appears; once he has been granted an interview with Melibea, the lover's forgetfulness is replaced by vigilance and he even chides his servants for their failure to watch the time — «¡O cómo me descontenta el oluido en los moços! De mi mucho acuerdo en esta noche e tu descuydar e oluido se haría vna razonable memoria e cuydado» (II. 76-77).

But Rojas never plays with a medieval topic without a purpose. At the same time that he grants Calisto his role as the most imaginative character of the work, Rojas underscores the lover's cowardice and his rationalization of the death of his servants. Memory is a device by which to escape guilt — «Ellos eran sobrados e esforzados: agora o en otro tiempo de pagar hauían. La vieja era mala e falsa, según parece que hazía trato con ellos, e assí que reñieron sobre la capa del justo. Permissión fue diuina que assí acabasse en pago de muchos adulterios que por su intercessión o causa son cometidos» (II. 112, Act XIII). In Act XIV Tristán and Sosia make the final ironic comment on «lover's forgetfulness», which Rojas can now transmute into a cynical selfishness and oblivion of human life:

> SOSIA: Para con tal joya quienquiera se ternía manos; pero con su pan se la coma, que bien caro le cuesta: dos moços entraron en la salsa destos amores.
> TRISTÁN: Ya los tiene oluidados. ¡Déxaos morir siruiendo a ruynes, hazed locuras en confiança de su defensión! Viuiendo con el Conde, que no matase al hombre, me daua mi madre por consejo. Veslos a ellos alegres e abraçados e sus seruidores con harta mengua degollados (II. 118-119).

Lover's forgetfulness becomes yet another mark of human isolation and the demythification of individual worth. As we will see, not even Celestina can escape this process.

E. CELESTINA, MEMORY, AND DEATH

Act XII marks that redefinition of memory as consciousness which we mentioned in the first pages of this study. Calisto and Melibea indirectly acknowledge in their colloquy that memory, for Rojas, is identified with all human experience and time-consciousness — that it is memory which binds each person to his surroundings and which symbolizes subjugation to time and causality, and that because of human blindness, memory will always fail in its rôle as the handmaiden of prudence. But the colloquy also suggests an escape from memory and time — the lover's oblivion caused, in Calisto's case, by the image of Melibea, and in Melibea's case, by Calisto's name. Calisto in particular is conscious of his attempt to use memory as a defense — «O quántos días antes de agora passados me fue venido este pensamiento a mi coraçón, e por impossible le recha-çaua de mi memoria» (II. 85). But ironically he thinks of his obli-vion as an awakening — «los rayos ylustrantes de tu muy claro gesto dieron luz en mis ojos, encendieron mi coraçón, despertaron mi len-gua...» (II. 85).

Pármeno and Sempronio, in the same act, practise another form of attempted escape from the lessons of memory. They learn how to manipulate memory for pragmatic purpose, a lesson taught them by Celestina. After their cowardly flight from imagined perils, they recall their younger years and lie about their 'heroism' of the past. This seals their pact of friendship through cowardice and deceit.

> PÁRMENO: Que nueue años seruí a los frayles de Guadalupe, que mill vezes nos apuñeávamos yo e otros. Pero nunca como esta vez houe miedo de morir.
> SEMPRONIO: E ¿yo no seruí al cura de Sant Miguel e al meso-nero de la plaça e a Mollejar, el ortelano? E también yo tenía mis questiones con los que tirauan piedras a los pájaros, que assentauan en un álamo grande que tenía, porque dañauan la ortaliza (II. 90). [25]

Pármeno and Sempronio, as we pointed out, formerly rejected memory; now they begin to understand how to use it to their own advantage. It is, however, too late for them. For Calisto's benefit they embroider the lies about their prowess — «Nunca me assenté ni avn junté por Dios los pies, mirando a todas partes para, en sin-tiendo porque [*Trag.*: poder], saltar presto e hazer todo lo que mis fuerças me ayudaran» (II. 93-94). But they cannot pull the wool over Celestina's eyes, for she is a much more skilful manipulator of memory. If they can lie about their bravery, she can invent a more fabulous lie — the chain which Calisto has given her has been lost. This false past is elaborated in great detail, and is camouflaged in the same dialogue form as her «true» memories — «Entraron vnos

---

[25] Gilman has pointed out the biographical significance of «Mollejar el orte-lano» — the Rojas family property at Montalbán was known as the «guerta de Mollegas» — and he has speculated that the incident related by Sempronio «is a per-sonal reminiscence drawn from Rojas' own childhood» (*Art.,* p. 218). It is curious that a true note from his past would be used by Rojas for a falsified reminiscence in one of the *Tragicomedia* interpolations. See also Gilman's article with F. del Valle Lersundi, «Mollejas el ortelano» in *Estudios dedicados a James Homer Herriott* (Madison, University of Wisconsin, 1966), 103-107.

conoscidos e familiares míos en aquella sazón aquí: temo no la ayan leuado, diziendo: si te vi, burléme, etc.» (II. 98).

Finally she claims credit for more courage than they — «Que si me ha dado algo, dos vezes he puesto por él mi vida al tablero. Más herramienta se me ha embotado en su seruicio que a vosotros, más materiales he gastado» (II. 99). And Pármeno is again reminded of his mother — «De lo qual fuera buen testigo su madre de Pármeno» (II. 99).

The memory of cowardice and the memory of Claudina enrage Sempronio and Pármeno. Celestina desperately tries the stratagem which had worked before with both: the bribe of women. But this time the offer falls on deaf ears. The tightly knit web of memory with which she had trapped her victims now ensnares Celestina. One more mention of cowardice, and the thought of Claudina, become unbearable to Sempronio and Pármeno.

> CELESTINA: E tú, Pármeno, no pienses que soy tu catiua por saber mis secretos e mi passada vida e los casos que nos acaescieron a mí e a la desdichada de tu madre. E avn assí me trataua ella, quando Dios quería.
> PÁRMENO: No me hinches las narizes con essas memorias (II. 102).
> ... ...
> CELESTINA: ...Señal es de gran couardía acometer a los menores e a los que poco pueden (II. 102-103).

This, for the servants of Calisto, is the last straw. Memory, like time, fortune, and love, has fatal powers in *La Celestina* and contributes to the fatal destinies of its victims.

The primitive author suggests the possibilities of memory to Rojas, but it is Rojas himself who transforms memory into a deep commentary on character. At the same time in Act XII that memory is recognized as a metaphor for all consciousness, Calisto and Melibea betray the lover's blindness which will lead them to their deaths, and Sempronio and Pármeno warp memory to use it as a shield against the truth. Even Celestina, who throughout has been the supreme ironic example of memory as Prudence, forgets herself and overplays her hand. She, who has used memory as a weapon, now finds that weapon twisting against her.

Thus, through the first twelve acts of the *Comedia*, memory has been transformed into an elaborate metaphor. On the one hand it has been the symbol of consciousness: Calisto and Melibea realize

41

this in Act XII, and Celestina, more than anyone else, exercises this freedom of memory to recreate a past glory and companionship which has gone forever. Memory has also been recognized as a prudent defense against the world and fortune — Pármeno for example has tried to use it in this fashion, and has failed. But there is an opposing force at work within the *Comedia* — the force of forgetfulness, oblivion, even falsification of memory, which ultimately breaks through the defensive barriers built by memory as consciousness. This oblivion is represented in various forms; the «lover's forgetfulness» which possesses Calisto; the forgetfulness of old age eaten away by time in Celestina and Alisa; the intentional ignoring of death by Calisto and Elicia in the additional acts. The prudence of memory as consciousness is overcome for the lovers by images and names which when remembered have an almost magical force: [26] recall Melibea's swoon at the mention of Calisto's name. In the case of Celestina herself it is caused internally — her own greed blinds her to the prudent manipulation of memory and brings her to the last fatal falsification, the lie about the chain. Her self-pride leads her to exceed the bounds of prudence in calling back the memories of Sempronio's cowardice and Pármeno's childhood. For Sempronio and Pármeno themselves it is falsification of past courage to lessen present cowardice — failure to face the truth in memory — that leads to their deaths. Even a minor character like Alisa is a victim of the forces of memory. Her failure to remember Celestina's true nature is tantamount to a betrayal of her daughter. If *memoria* is redefined as consciousness in *La Celestina,* then *oluido* must be seen as a symbol of death. The irony is that both have fatal powers.

---

[26] For the power of names and the spoken word in the Spanish Middle Ages, see Leo Spitzer, «Los romances españoles», in *Sobre antigua poesía española* (Buenos Aires, 1962).

III. MEMORY AND TIME IN THE *COMEDIA*

A. The «Comedia» and Aristotelian Time

In recent works of criticism, time has been one of the most thoroughly discussed aspects of *La Celestina*. In Cejador's view, the inconsistency of exterior chronology (four days) and the passage of time as it is felt by the various characters could be explained by the inconsistency of the author of the additions. [1] This inadequate explanation has been rejected in recent criticism. Manuel Asensio and Stephen Gilman have polarized the contemporary discussion of time in *La Celestina*. [2] The latter pointed out «Rojas' failure to equate the duration of the individual life with external time» *(Art,* p. 146), or the difference between duration and dimension. María Rosa Lida de Malkiel concluded brilliantly that «La acción representada en *La Celestina* no es, pues, la secuencia ininterrumpida de la realidad, sino una muestra típica de su serie» *(Originalidad,* p. 179). In other words, Rojas does not maintain an uninterrupted time sequence, but includes in his acts a representative sampling of the interior development of the characters. The three time sequences existing in *La Celestina* are that of actual speech, that perceived or experienced by the speakers, and that inferred from the dialogue.

It is not difficult to justify a discussion of time on the grounds of its intimate relation with memory; indeed, a sense of time in the characters would be virtually impossible without memory. Sempronio's first memory in Act I begins «Días ha grándes que

---

[1] More recently Laurent Teixidor has returned to this viewpoint *(Observations sur La Celestina,* Périgueux, 1968, pp. 25-27).

[2] See Asensio's articles, «El tiempo y el género literario en *La Celestina*» *RFH* VII (1945), 147-159, and «El tiempo en *La Celestina, HR* XX (1952), 28-43, and Gilman's reply, *HR* XXI (1953), 42-45.

conosco en fin desta vezindad vna vieja barbuda, que se dize Celestina...» (I. 58). It is, however, more difficult to justify yet another contribution to what seems an already glutted market. But one area seems to have been somewhat overlooked. What would have been the contemporary influences on Rojas' own concept of time? From an examination of the temporal theories prevalent in the universities of the day, a pattern begins to emerge. The two pillars in the late medieval university, including Rojas' own university of Salamanca, were Aristotelianism and Stoicism. Although the Stoicism of Seneca and Petrarch was dominant in the late fifteenth century, Aristotle's works remained an extremely important part of the university curriculum. Yet, returning to *La Celestina*, Aristotelian influence in the work has inspired little interest, when compared to the many comments on Rojas' use of Petrarch. As Castro Guisasola pointed out, virtually all the Aristotelian passages occur in the unknown author's first act. [3] Gilman noted his presence only in Act I «with characters who are not yet fully engaged in conflict, not yet involved vitally in dialogic situations» (*Art,* p. 170). And although María Rosa Lida de Malkiel remarked on Aristotelian influences, Aristotle was not a central figure in her analysis of the book.

Yet the influence of Aristotle extends beyond the quotations noted in the first act. Aristotelian causality is implied by Pármeno in his «Señor, por perderse el otro día el neblí» speech in Rojas' second act. But perhaps more interesting is Pármeno's «No curo de lo que dizes, porque en los bienes mejor es el acto que la potencia e en los males mejor la potencia que el acto» (I. 97, Act I). [4] This garbled fragment of schoolboy philosophy also brings to mind the Aristotelian theory of motion — «Motus est actus entis in po-

---

[3] He concludes that he probably was familiar with Aristotle's *Physica, De caelo et mundi, Ethica, Magna Moral., Metaphysica.* He notes that the only possible attributions to Aristotle after Act I occur in Act IV («El perro con todo su ímpetu e braueza, quando viene a morder, si se le echan en el suelo no haze mal», *Rhetorica),* and Act VII («Ninguna cosa ay criada al mundo superflua») a line often quoted by Aristotle in *De caelo, Politica,* etc. *(Observaciones sobre las fuentes literarias de La Celestina,* RFE Anejo V, Madrid, 1924, pp. 23-24).

[4] The ultimate source of this is book IX of the *Metaphysica* — «Quod autem (in bonis) melior ac praestantior quam ipsa boni potentia, actus sit, ex his patebat: quaecumque enim secundum posee dicuntur, idem est potens contraria: ut quod dicitur posse sanum esse, idem est etiam aegrotans, et simul eadem potentia est sanum et aegrotum esse. Actus igitur melior (in bonis). Necesse autem est etiam in malis finem et actum deteriorem potentia esse» (Castro Guisasola, p. 27).

tentia secundum quod in potentia est», where Aristotelian «motion» includes movement through what we would now call both space and time — «Motion denotes any transition from potentiality to actuality, whether this change be generation or corruption of a substantial form, whether it be alteration in quality or in quantity, or whether it refers to occupation of a different place (local motion in the narrow sense).» [5]

If Rojas (and the primitive author) did hold the Aristotelian view of motion, then a solution of the much-discussed problem of duration and dimension in *La Celestina* may be possible. To postulate that Rojas saw little difference between movement in time and space is not to call him ingenuous; it was an inevitable result of his training in Aristotelian thought. Gerald Holton in his description of Aristotelian theory as the «allegory of motion», points out that:

> The representation of motion in its full allegorical sense is therefore as impossible in science as it is in painting, or, for that matter, in a literary work. The need to use civilized mathematical functions is incongruous with respect to the discontinuous nature of self-conscious experience; and conversely, the need to take data during experimentation is incongruous with respect to the continuous nature of the processes which are being investigated (p. 196).

The «muestra típica» of reality is then the only method which an Aristotelian can employ to give a sampling from the unending flow of movement. The paradoxical «times» of *La Celestina,* which have been seen as a clash between external dimension (the four-day action of the work) and internal duration (the much longer psychological process of the love affair), are resolved when they become a function of motion. Rojas as author cannot catalogue every moment of the physical and psychological development of the love affair; instead he gives us a sampling of both. Although he seemingly presents an unbroken sequence of events, we realize that this surface unity is illusory; while maintaining the illusion of continuous surface motion he is in fact giving us a sampling of both physical and psychological motion and time which extends over a month or more.

---

[5] Gerald Holton, «Science and the Changing Allegory of Motion», *Scientia* XCVIII (1963), 191.

This is scarcely a discovery of the twentieth century. Rodrigo Vasurto, a renowned teacher at Salamanca in the 1490's, had already said much the same in his *De natura loci et temporis.* Whether the young Rojas actually attended this lecture series is unimportant. Given the prevailing influence of Aristotelianism, all the evidence points to the fact that Vasurto would have been voicing current philosophical opinion when he said:

> Dignus est igitur concludere cum auicena qui tam diserte et sapiente locutus est in hoc et dicere que tempus habeat esse in res natura et similiter motus. Cum enim factus fuerit aliquis motus verum est dicere que fuit nunquam tamen verum fuit dicere que est nam cum nos sumus in esse permanenti et intellectus noster intelligat in instanti: cum affirmamus aliquid esse vel fuisse vel futurus esse: locutio nostra trahitur ad indiuisible in quo sumus. [6]

Vasurto's analysis of the «esse permanenti» is in fact central to Rojas' understanding of the relation of his characters to time and memory; the past and the future collide in the present voices of *La Celestina.*

As proof of Rojas' familiarity with the Aristotelian theory of motion, one need only examine the inventory of his library, which contained the Spanish transliteration and allegorization of Maimonides' *Guide to the Perplexed,* the «Visión delectable de la filosofía y artes liberales, metafísica y filosofía moral; compuesto por Alfonso de la Torre, bachiller». [7] Under the heading of Chapter X, there is

---

[6] Salamanca, 1494 (in the library of The Hispanic Society), fol. Diii recto: Therefore it is worthy to agree with Avicena who has spoken so clearly and wisely about this matter, and so to say that time has an existence among the things of nature, and, at the same time, motion. For when some motion *will be done,* it is true to say that it never *has been,* but it has been truly said that it *is;* for when we have a permanent being, and our intellect undertands in the present moment, when we affirm something *to be* or *to have been* or *to be about to be,* our speech is brought back to the indivisible condition in which we are.

[7] Valle Lersundi, «Testamento». It is interesting to note that as late as 1592, Fray Hernando de Zárate used the metaphor of motion to express biological time, in his «Discursos de la paciencia cristiana»:

> Pues la divina Escritura nos pinta como justadores con la muerte con gran velocidad; porque de nosotros dice que partimos para ello como un arroyo de agua o río, el cual vemos que corre con tanta velocidad, que apenas se conoce

a discussion of Aristotelian motion, containing the precept, «Todo tiempo acompaña al movimiento, et no se puede fallar uno sin otro.» [8] Maimonides himself was more prolix on this topic:

> Even time itself is among the things created; for time depends on motion, i. e. on an accident in things which move, and the things upon whose motion time depends are themselves created beings which have passed from nonexistence... For time is undoubtedly an accident, and according to our opinion, one of the created accidents, like blackness and whiteness; it is not a quality, but an accident connected with motion. This must be clear to all who understand what Aristotle has said on time and its real existence. [9]

The presence of Aristotelian time-space theory within the *Comedia* may be verified by examining Sempronio's well-known speech about time and forgetfulness:

> Que no ay cosa tan difícile de çofrir en sus principios, que el tiempo no la ablande e faga comportable... El mal e el bien, la prosperidad e aduersidad, la gloria e pena, todo pierde con el tiempo la fuerça de su acelerado principio... Cada día vemos nouedades e las oymos e las passamos e dexamos atrás. Diminúyelas el tiempo, házelas contingibles... Todo es assí, todo passa desta manera, todo se oluida, todo queda atrás... Que la costumbre luenga amansa los dolores, afloxa e deshaze los deleytes, desmengua las marauillas. Procuremos prouecho, mientra pendiere la contienda (I. 129-132, Act III).

When Sempronio says — «Todo *passa* desta manera... todo queda *atrás*» (p. 132) he applies the rhetoric of motion to time. «Cada día vemos nouedades... e las *passamos* e *dexamos atrás*» (p. 129).

---

en la tierra otro mayor; porque aunque un río vaya manso al parecer... el agua sin duda va con gran velocidad... Así es la vida del hombre, que mirada a lo que parece va de espacio; de manera que se pasan diez, veinte, cuarenta años sin que en la vida de un mancebo se eche de ver mudanza; pero en realidad va corriendo velocísima como el río. (MAE 27, Madrid, 1853, p. 518.)

[8]   Ed. Adolfo de Castro in *Curiosidades bibliográficas,* BAE 36 (Madrid, 1855), p. 353.
[9]   Moses Maimonides, *The Guide for the Perplexed,* trans. M. Friedlander (New York, 1956), p. 171.

The physical and biological world of human ageing is leagued with the abstract notion of «time». [10] Celestina will rail against death — «Por vno, que *comes* con tiempo, cortas mil en agraz» (I. 135, Act III). The «teeth of time» is the physical metaphor for the biological process of time. «El mal e el bien, la prosperidad e aduersidad, la gloria e pena, todo pierde con el tiempo *la fuerça de su acelerado principio*» (p. 129; my italics). Even abstract qualities move physically through time, united with their human counterparts. Aristotelian time-space defines a biological world which begins with a burst, an «acelerado principio», that then slows down through spatial inertia and temporal decay. This slowing-down process is visible in the structure of *La Celestina*. The first dramatic confrontation of Calisto and Melibea in the garden is the prelude to a long series of visitations by Celestina. The matter of Pármeno slows her first visits to Calisto and Melibea; the banqueting scene decelerates the second round of visits even further, and forward movement is virtually halted by the assignations and deaths in the sixteen-act version. The tempo of the additional acts serves as an additional brake by introducing yet another rendezvous and the Centurio subplot. Finally, the two long laments provide a suitable conclusion to the process.

Celestina is the human representative of this process of deceleration within the work — «Mi honrra llegó a la cumbre, según quien yo era: de necessidad es que desmengüe e se abaxe. Cerca ando de mi fin. En esto veo que me queda poca vida» (II. 44, Act IX). Physical number and physical appearance also reflect the reduction — her «nueue moças de tus días» have now been reduced to two. Elsewhere she says «Señora, ten tú el tiempo que no ande; terné yo mi forma que no se mude» (I. 171, Act IV). «La ley es de fortuna que ninguna cosa en vn ser mucho tiempo permanesce» (II. 44, Act IX) — again the Aristotelian theory of motion and

---

[10] Gilman had already perceived the close relationship of time and space in Sempronio's speech (*Art.*, p. 135):

> There is only one significant difference between this presentation of time and that of the 'ubi sunt' commonplace of previous years. In the latter, time passes by objects, atmospheres, and men, while for Sempronio time joins life from within, causing the individual to forget past evaluations and excitements. Preoccupation with time joins preoccupation with space at the roots of the consciousness of being alive.

change.   Alfonso de la Torre summarizes the entire argument briefly in the *Visión delectable:*

> Son los movimientos o mutaciones en la sustancia, generación et corrupción; en la cuantidad, augmento et diminución; según la cualidad, alteración; según el lugar, mudamiento del fine o lugar (p. 353).

As for the entire structure of the sixteen-act *Celestina,* Pármeno defines the «accelerado principio» early in Act II — «Señor, porque perderse el otro día el neblí fue causa de tu entrada en la huerta de Melibea a le buscar, la entrada causa de la ver e hablar, la habla engendró amor, el amor parió tu pena, la pena causará perder tu cuerpo e alma e hazienda» (I. 121).   It is the «amor» and «pena», abetted by Celestina (often called the «primum mobile» of the work) that slows down the vital structure of the work (even more so in the twenty-one act version).   But time is not allowed to decelerate the biological life naturally;   natural change is suddenly replaced by violent change in the deaths of the main characters — «Todo mudamiento, o es natural, así como el descendimiento de la cosa pesada ayuso; o es violento, así como cuando lanzan la saeta o piedra hacia arriba» (Alfonso de la Torre, p. 353).

Memory emerges as the representative of consciousness in this external world of Aristotelian time-space.   It is through memory and forgetfulness that the characters of *La Celestina* attempt to manipulate the external world to serve their own ends.   As Calisto realizes in Act XIV, internal time fails to correspond to time in its external manifestations;   and so the internal world of memory will be an evasion, an attempt to cheat reality.   Celestina's consciousness lives in a distant past;   the world of the present does not have the same impact on her, and she forgets recent occurrences.   Yet she will use her memories of the past to influence Pármeno, Calisto, Melibea, Lucrecia.   Sempronio, Pármeno, Calisto all live for the present or the future.   Sempronio acknowledges no past, only the present;   Pármeno rejects the past that he remembers;   Calisto as the oblivious lover has neither past nor present, only future.   These different qualities of memory correspond to their ages as well as to their rôles in the drama.   Celestina underscores the differences with the admonition to the young lovers — «Gozá vuestras frescas mocedades, que quien tiempo tiene e mejor le espera, tiempo viene que se arrepiente. Como yo hago agora por algunas horas que dexé perder, quando moça, quando me preciaua, quando me querían. Que ya ¡mal pecado! caducado he, nadie no me quiere» (II, 39, Act IX). Rojas acknowledges that the manner in which we remember is one of the main determinants of character, and that memory is the filter of consciousness. But as a good Aristotelian, he also shows that the attempts to impose subjective experience on the relentless movement of an impersonal universe not only fail, but in several cases lay the groudwork for self-destruction. Memory, as we have already seen in Act XII, far from providing an escape, will converge like time and space on death.

B. TIME AND THE DEATH OF MELIBEA

«Gozá vuestras frescas mocedades» — these words will be recast by Melibea after the death of Calisto — «¿Cómo no gozé más del gozo? ¿Cómo tuue en tan poco la gloria que entre mis manos toue? ¡O ingratos mortales! ¡Jamás conocés vuestros bienes, sino quando dellos carescéys!» (II. 186, Act XIX). The irrevocable power of the past; the failure of memory even to bring solace — these themes enter the last two acts of *La Celestina*. Violent death has all but destroyed the forward motion of the drama (a motion which after the death of Celestina has to be resuscitated by Elicia and Areúsa); the two survivors, Melibea and Pleberio, acknowledge that time has stopped for them. Violent death has, in fact, upset natural order, and Rojas having reached the limit of the Aristotelian time-chain, now moves farther. He reaches out beyond Aristotle's cosmic order, and his concept of «natures». As Alexandre Koyré explains: «Movement is necessarily a transitory state; natural movement ends naturally when it reaches its goal. As for violent movement, Aristotle is too optimistic to admit that this abnormal status could endure. moreover, violent movement is disorder creating disorder, and to admit that it could endure indefinitely would mean, in fact, to abandon the very idea of a well-ordered Cosmos. Aristotle, therefore, holds the reassuring belief that nothing which is *contra naturam possit esse perpetuum*.» [11] But Pleberio will rail against fortune and the world: «*Turbóse la orden* del morir con la tristeza

---

[11] «Galileo and Plato», *Journal of the History of Ideas*, IV (1943), 409.

que te aquexaua...» (II. 202, Act XX). «Dexárasme aquella florida planta, en quien tú poder no tenías; diérasme, fortuna fluctuosa, triste la mocedad con vegez alegre, no *peruertieras la orden...*» (II. 203). «Yo pensaua en mi más tierna edad que eras y eran tus hechos regidos por *alguna orden;* agora visto el pro e la contra de tus bienandanças, me pareces vn laberinto de errores...» (II, 204; my italics). Here is Rojas' world of perspectivism, in which man suddenly discovers his insignificance and helplessness. Rojas' carefully constructed Aristotelian chain of events has resulted in a violence which destroys all order and leaves the survivors, Melibea and Pleberio, in an Aristotelian absurdity — in a world without time or space; in a void. Thus, finally, Rojas' cynicism destroys even the idea that memory can serve as a guard against the vicissitudes of the world. Pleberio's prudence is, in the final analysis, of no more value in fending off disaster than Melibea and Calisto's *olvido.* Pleberio recognizes this fact in his bitter condemnation of love; «Bien pensé que de tus lazos me auía librado, quando los quarenta años toqué, quando fui contento con mi conjugal compañera, quando me vi con el fruto que me cortaste el día de oy. No pensé que tomauas en los hijos la vengança de los padres» (II. 209).

Melibea's consciousness has depended on living from moment to moment; now she is imprisoned, left without past or future: «Tú, Señor, que de mi habla eres testigo, ves mi poco poder, ves quán catiua tengo mi libertad, quán presos mis sentidos de tan poderoso amor del muerto cauallero, que priua al que tengo con los viuos padres» (II. 194, Act XIX). The death of consciousness means the death of memory and imagination — even her formal memory of «casos de antigüedad» is a feeble attempt to escape guilt for the probable demise of her parents after her death — «Éstos son digno de culpa, éstos son verdaderos parricidas, que no yo...» (II. 193).

Melibea's farewell to her father is a dry and factual account of her relations with Calisto; her only flight into imagination a sorrowful future which she will never see, but for which she accepts the blame. «Yo cobrí de luto e xergas en este día quasi la mayor parte de la cibdadana cauallería... yo quité a los viuos el dechado de gentileza, de inuenciones galanas, de atauíos e bordaduras, de habla, de andar, de cortesía, de virtud...» (II. 195-196). This description is tantamount to the *ubi sunt* of Manrique's *Coplas.* Finally her account of Calisto's death is a brutal description: «De la triste cayda sus

más escondidos sesos quedaron repartidos por las piedras e paredes»
(II. 197). Melibea's death is neither imitation (except for its manner) nor divine retribution; it is, rather, the only option for a person
stranded outside of time.

Pleberio is left behind, in total temporal and physical isolation.
His successful past has been rendered meaningless by the death of his
only daughter; his future no longer exists without an heir and
companion... «quanto tiempo me dexare solo después de ti, fálteme
la vida, pues me faltó tu agradable compañía... ¡Oh duro coraçón
de padre! ¿Cómo no te quiebras de dolor, que ya quedas sin tu amada
heredera? ¿Para quién edifiqué torres? ¿Para quién adquirí hon-
rras? ¿Para quién planté árboles? ¿Para quién fabriqué nauíos?»
(II. 202). The past and the memory of the past have lost all
value for Pleberio, and when he berates the world for its false
hopes and happiness, even his stock memory of Stoic *exempla* fails
him entirely — «Yo fui lastimado sin hauer ygual compañero de
semejante dolor; avnque más en mi *fatigada memoria* rebueluo presentes e passados» (II. 205-206; my italics). Pericles, Xenophon,
Anaxagoras, David all had some consolation for their losses.

Fortune and time can no longer have any influence on Pleberio
and he consoles himself with the Petrarchan rationale — «Agora
perderé contigo, mi desdichada hija, los miedos e temores que cada
día me espauorecían: sola tu muerte es la que a mí me haze seguro
de sospecha» (II. 208, Act XX). Those real memories of the
past which still exist in the «fatigada memoria» of Pleberio now
seem like a punishment. And he bitterly completes Pármeno's
recognition of destructive causality which brings an evil end to the
love affair. «¿En qué pararon tus siruientes e sus ministros? La
falsa alcahueta Celestina murió a manos de los más fieles compañeros
que ella para tu seruicio empoçoñado jamás halló. Ellos murieron
degollados, Calisto, despeñado. Mi triste hija quiso tomar la misma
muerte por seguirle. Esto todo causas» (II. 210). Finally he
complains that this movement was irrevocable — «Del mundo me
quexo, porque en sí me crió, porque no me dando vida, no engendra-
ra en él a Melibea; no nascida, no amara; no amando, cessara mi
quexosa e desconsolada postrimería» (II. 211).

So the past, retrievable only through memory, disappears in pain.
The future exists no longer for Pleberio, least responsible for but
most punished by the inescapable destruction of time. The present
must end when dialogue is cut off and monologue fails. The micro-

cosm of humanity and time has destroyed itself in *La Celestina,*
leaving Pleberio «triste e solo in hac lachrymarum valle». When
his monologue in the void ends, Pleberio too disappears without
a trace.

C. TIME AND CHARACTER

By now it is clear that time was implicit in our discussion of
memory and character in Chapter II. There, Celestina was the
antagonist of time, Sempronio the advocate of time's healing effects.
We noted the reactions of Pleberio's household to the passage of
time, as well as the forgetfulness of time both in the young and the
old. Time, which plays a central part in memory, also is central
to an understanding of character.

Specific reference to time in memory by the personae of *La Celestina* can be analysed in the light of character, and the most
interesting fact deduced from the raw statistics of time quotations
is that while Celestina is the character who thinks in the most
specific fashion of time, her sense of time is much further in the past.
She refers to past time usually in terms of years: «sesenta años»
(II. 102), veynte e tres años» (I. 186), «diez e seys» (I. 241),
«quatro años» (I. 226). When referring to shorter intervals, she
speaks in terms of days, never hours or the hour of the clock
(although once she admits it is getting late), and aims these references
at her younger audience to indicate passage of time — Calisto has
had his toothache for a week or eight days (I. 187), a long time
to Melibea; but she has known Pármeno's whereabouts for only three
days (half a week), a short time to Pármeno, the only young member
of the cast who recalls distant occurrences and cites them in years.
However, Sempronio's absence of three days is a long time, for
diplomatic reasons (I. 61). The other main «rememberer», Pármeno,
speaks in terms of «nueue años» (II. 90), «seys dozenas de años»
(I. 126), «días grandes» (I. 69). He generally only speaks of more
inmediate time when it concerns Areúsa or his cowardice, and time
suddenly becomes desperately short — «Bien se te acordará, no ha
mucho que me prometiste que me harías hauer a Areúsa» (I. 245);
«Ya ha dos horas que te requiero que nos vamos, que no faltará vn
achaque» (II. 87). Sempronio, ironic and oblivious of time, perceives it only occasionally and in its smallest units, of day and hour

(he has been awaiting Celestina since one o'clock, I. 196), unless of course he wants to establish his authority — «Días ha grandes que conosco en fin desta vezindad vna vieja barbuda...» (I. 58).

The contrast between «practical» rememberers, both young and old, on the one hand, and Calisto and Melibea on the other is enormous. Celestina, Pármeno, and Sempronio aim their memories for effect at least as much as they reveal their character through the type of memory. By contrast, Calisto and Melibea are ingenuous rememberers — their pasts extend only from the beginning of the work, with the single exception of Melibea's previous knowledge of Celestina, which reveals how slowly time moves for her. For Melibea it is always «Muchos e muchos días» (II. 61) since she has first seen Calisto, or has been falling in love with him (II. 86), or since he has been her lover (II. 196) — even though in the last case, we are told that the time has not been much more than a month.

Calisto shares this trait — he refers to the period before his first assignation with Melibea in terms of «tantas noches» (I. 219), «quantos días» (II. 85), and of the period of their love as «toda mi vida» (II. 117). After their first meeting in the garden it seems like only one hour that he has spent with her (II. 119), but when he has to wait for the second rendezvous, «paresce... un año» (II, 128). And as María Rosa Lida de Malkiel observed, his perception of hour of the day only begins when the first assignation is in sight (II. 76-77). [12] Thus both lovers expand and contract time in response to internal consciousness, rather than to external necessity.

An examination of the units of time mentioned throughout the work by the personae yields the identical conclusion that time, even time objectively expressed, is a fluid notion which reflects internal consciousness or external necessity. Thus time in terms of hours can seem short or long to the speakers — for Calisto it is only four short hours since he has seen his servants, now dead (II. 109); for Pármeno it is two endless hours that he and Sempronio have been

---

[12] *Originalidad*, p. 170. She also observes «parece que los enamorados tuviesen un sentido infinitesimal del tiempo, que hace especialmente dolorosos los últimos minutos de cada espera». This lengthening of time was a commonplace in both the popular and cultured lyric and numerous examples are listed under the «insomnia» topic in E. M. Torner's *Lírica hispánica* (Madrid, 1966), no. 198, pp. 347-351. The best known of these is «Estas noches atán largas / para mí / no solían ser ansí», which received a cultivated treatment by Juião Bolseiro in the *Cancioneiro da Vaticana* («Aquestas noytes tam longas»).

waiting for the lovers' assignation to end (II. 87). The main units of time mentioned in *La Celestina* are three days (half a week), eight days (a week), a month, a year, two years, four years, nine years and sixteen years. Three and eight days are most frequently mentioned, and expand or contract with consciousness and necessity, as already seen with Celestina. For Areúsa, it is only a feu nights that she has had with Pármeno (II. 138); for Elicia it is a brief three days before the «virgin» to be mended is married (I. 261). Areúsa has seen Pármeno and Sempronio alive only eight days before (II. 136), but Calisto has had a toothache for eight long days (I. 187). The four years that Celestina lived near Pleberio's household is a long time (I. 226), but her sixteen-year acquaintance with Claudina seems all too brief (I. 241). The most important new note of time introduced by the additional acts will be the unit of «un mes», that same month of Calisto and Melibea's love, of Pleberio's and Alisa's decision to marry off Melibea, of the collapse of Celestina's prosperous house. María Rosa Lida de Malkiel pointed out that *El Tractado de Centurio* usa con mayor libertad y claridad del tiempo implícito, de acciones que se han cumplido sin haberse representado» *(Originalidad,* p. 176). This month is, in fact, the only large unit of time (other than specific hours of the clock) that has an objective reality as well as subjective one in the work. [13]

Thus we can make one further alteration to the notion of the time-sequences of *La Celestina*. The Aristotelian theory of motion has solved the problem of the clash between the four-day action of the play and the psychological process of the love affair. But Rojas' understanding of time as motion has proved to be even more radical — time has become a reflection of the internal tempo of the characters in *La Celestina,* and of their personal trajectories. There are not just two or three time-sequences in *La Celestina,* but a proliferation of times, interwoven according to persons and moods.

---

[13] Even Celestina's various mentions of «years passed» cannot be considered objectively reliable; recall the conflicting opinions of her age. And certainly this «month» of the «Tractado» is the only objective unit of time operating *within* the work.

IV. *LA CELESTINA,* MEMORY, AND GENRE

A. Memory, Imagination and Genre in the Additional Acts

When Stephen Gilman stated that *La Celestina* is ageneric, he based his conclusion on «the apparent lack of authorial participation in the presentation of speaker and listener» *(Art,* p. 201); in other words, on the lack of the third person. For him, the pure dialogic form of *La Celestina,* its exclusive *tú* and *yo,* leads to the creation of human lives which cannot be called «novelistic» because they lack external reality and existence. One of the purposes of the study so far has been to show that this external reality does indeed exist in *La Celestina.* This is not to revert to the tired argument that the work is a «novela dramática»; rather, it is an attempt to reestablish Rojas as a precursor of the novel, as the first Spanish author to use memory as the bridge between the subjective and objective realities of his characters. Our examination of the sixteen-act *Comedia* has yielded a series of observations which fit Lukács' definition of the novel. [1] Rojas has developed a concept of memory as the key to consciousness; memory projects his characters into an imaginative time dimension in which present embraces past and future. Furthermore, memory passages supply an «objective» reality for *La Celestina* — even those characters which lack the objectively described background of Celestina seem to enjoy an implied background in memory (Melibea's pre-adolescence, Sempronio's childhood education, etc.). The perspectivism which is often involved in this objective reality only heightens the relationship between the inner and outer worlds — how the *mochachas* see Melibea, and how Ca-

---

[1] See p. 8, above.

listo sees her in memory, are keys to the personalities of the observers.

As for the additional acts, we have already pointed out one «novelistic» development — the emergence of an objective unit of time, the month of love. It has already been suggested that the added acts of La Celestina evolve toward fiction and drama; [2] memory will play a central role in the evolution as early as Act XIII. Memory will tend to be transformed into imagination on the one hand, [3] or into a factual third-person narrative on the other, which often fails to transcend theatrical exposition. At the beginning of Act XIII, Calisto recalls his first interview with Melibea and wonders, «¿Soñélo o no? ¿Fue fantaseado o passó en verdad?» (II. 106). Calisto will become the artist of memory, refashioning it as a world of imagination. But at the same time, in the interpolations of Act XIII Sosia gives a purely factual description of the deaths of Sempronio and Pármeno:

> Ya sin sentido yuan; pero el uno con harta difficultad, como me sintió que con lloro le miraua, hincó los ojos en mí, alçando las manos al cielo, quasi dando gracias a Dios e como preguntándome qué [some eds.: si me] sentía de su morir (II. 108).

This is an almost «novelistic» memory technique, a description of recent action, occuring specifically and drawing the speaker into a personal relationship with the actor. However, location and ambience are not described, only the glances and movements of the condemned man. Rojas is still principally interested in human reality: the working of the mind as expressed through action and words.

---

[2] Gilman perceives in the additional acts «the first tentative fissures in the dialogue, the first hesitant segregation of novel and drama» (Art., p. 202). For María Rosa Lida de Malkiel, the Tractado de Centurio is one of the mainstays for her argument that the Tragicomedia is related to the classical Latin elegiac and humanistic comedies (Originalidad, pp. 29-50).

[3] One must be careful not to confuse imagination in its modern acceptance of «invention» with the «imagination and fantasy» which were two of the five inward senses (with memory, estimation, and common sense). C. S. Lewis says of these medieval «wits»: «According to Albertus, Imagination merely retains what has been perceived, and Phantasy deals with this componendo et dividendo, separating and uniting» (The Discarded Image, Cambridge, 1964, p. 163). Frances A. Yates has further clarified the medieval definition of imagination by pointing out its association with the storing of memory images (The Art of Memory, pp. 32ff.)

The interpolations to act XIV in the twenty-one act *Celestina* continue to explore the realms of memory and imagination, setting up the ironic counterpoint of apprehension and the rationalization of cowardice, versus the «ennobling» effects of love on imagination and memory. Melibea and Sosia are harbingers of this development; she sets her imagination to work when she worries about the possible evil fate of Calisto, using the stylistic techniques of memory:

> ¿O si por acaso los ladradores perros con sus crueles dientes, que ninguna differencia saben hazer ni acatamiento de personas, le ayan mordido? ¿O si ha caydo en alguna calçada o hoyo, donde algún daño le viniesse? ¡Mas, o mezquina de mí! ¿Qué son estos inconuenientes, que el concebido amor me pone delante e los atribulados ymaginamientos me acarrean? (II. 115).

This imaginative worrying about her absent lover may be seen as an offshoot of the type of very immediate worries that Celestina revealed in her monologue of Act IV, while approaching Pleberio's house.

Sosia expresses the same unrest later in Act XIV when he gives Tristán a panorama of the possible dangers awaiting them in the streets — «porque suelen leuantarse a esta hora los ricos, los cobdiciosos de temporales bienes, los deuotos de templos, monesterios e yglesias, los enamorados como nuestro amo, los trabajadores de los campos e labranças» (II. 121).

These passages might be called «foreshadowing», but they represent a new technique; the crowded external world now enters the imagination of the characters as well as their memory. Previously, imagined fears have been mentioned only in passing — Elicia's fear that some ill may befall Celestina in the streets; Celestina's own fear of falling. It is left for Calisto to elaborate this new trend; memory and imagination intensify both his cowardice over his dishonor and his poetic powers as a lover. «No sé si lo causa que me vino a la memoria la traycíon que fize en me despartir de aquella señora que tanto amo, hasta que más fuera de día, o el dolor de mi deshonrra» (II. 122, Act XIV). At first his fears win out; after a remarkable imaginary conversation with the judge who condemned Pármeno and Sempronio, he expands his own theory of time and causality — «Mayormente que no ay hora cierto ni limitada ni avn vn solo momento. Deudores somos sin tiempo, contino

59

estamos obligados a pagar luego» (II. 123). [4]   But he returns to his
senses — again the dreaming theme appears — «¿Pero qué digo?
¿Con quién hablo? ¿Estoy en mi seso?   ¿Qué es esto, Calisto?
¿Soñauas, duermes o velas?» (II. 125).   After a catalogue of Stoic
exempla, he forces himself to remember Melibea — «acuérdate, Calisto, del gran gozo passado.   Acuérdate de tu señora e tu bien todo»
(II. 127).

Calisto then conducts a monologue about time; perhaps he can
escape it yet — « ¡O luziente Febo, date priessa a tu acostumbrado
camino!   ¡O deleytosas estrellas, aparéceos ante de la continua orden!   ¡O espacioso relox, avn te vea yo arder en biuo fuego de
amor! » (II. 128).   But time is physically inescapable — «Todo se
rige con vn freno ygual, todo se mueue con igual espuela: cielo, tierra,
mar, fuego, viento, calor, frío.   ¿Qué me aprouecha a mí que dé
doze horas el relox de hierro, si no las ha dado el del cielo?   Pues,
por mucho que madrugue, no amanesce más ayna» (II. 128-129).
Time (though inescapable physically), may be evaded only through
memory and imagination.   Rojas grasps the essence of human
consciousness as a means both to evade and intensify reality;   this
limited escape is the only one open to men:

> Pero tú, dulce ymaginación, tú que puedes, me acorre. Trae a
> mi fantasía la presencia angélica de aquella ymagen luziente;
> buelue a mis oydos el suaue son de sus palabras, aquellos desuíos
> sin gana, aquel apártate allá, señor, no llegues a mí... (II. 129) [5].

Thus memory develops a new power in the additional acts — not
only can the characters mold their memory, as always, for their own

---

[4]   Calisto makes use of Petrarch *(Epistolae familiares);* see Castro Guisasola,
p. 130.

[5]   Much has been made of this passage by the outstanding critics. María Rosa
Lida de Malkiel calls Calisto's predicament «conflicto cosmológico y psicológico:
lo que tortura a Calisto es la marcha regular del cosmos, marcada ingeniosamente
por las manecillas sobre el cuadrante sin tomar en cuenta la arbitrariedad del alma
humana. Y entre la regularidad del mundo exterior y el ímpetu del deseo, no hay
para Calisto otro puente que revivir el pasado en la memoria y anticipar el futuro
en la 'dulce ymaginación', esto es, burlar la espera; anular el tiempo» *(Originalidad,*
p. 173). Although Gilman believes that it is Rojas' irony which operates when
Calisto believes himself free of time *(Art.,* pp. 138-139), he sees in Calisto's memory of the night of love an attempt to recapture *gozo* (the joining and communion
of two souls), which he considers the only antidote to Rojas' usual dark pessimism
(«Fernando de Rojas as Author», 278-288).

benefit and the benefit of others, but Calisto discovers the means of combining memory and imagination to escape time entirely. The cardboard Melibea of Act I has been transmuted in Calisto's memory, and the passage owes its style to the indirect dialogue techniques developed through the *Comedia*. Taking the conclusions one step further, this passage of the *Tragicomedia* begins to resemble the modern novel in its stream-of-consciousness technique. Although Aristotelian causality is still inescapable and rigid for Calisto, the human consciousness discovers a new space and time continuum within itself. [6]

A counterpoint to Calisto's development in the added acts is Melibea's personal development. In Act XVI her sense of the importance of the moment is contrasted with Pleberio's «No hay cosa tan ligera para huyr como la vida. La muerte nos sigue e rodea, de la qual somos vezinos e hazia su vandera nos acostamos, según natura» (II. 144). He, of course, fails to realize just how true this truism will become. Pleberio's experience of the flow of time and life is followed by Melibea's heightened perception of momentary *gozo* — «No tengo otra lástima sino por el tiempo que perdí de no gozarlo, de no conoscerlo, después que a mí me sé conoscer» (II. 148). Areúsa had already spoken these words — «desde que me sé conoscer» (II. 41, Act IX) — but Areúsa's world of the moment is sterile and lonely; she is isolated by personal pride. Melibea, by contrast, has learned to live for another. Like Calisto, time only matters for her when she is in her lover's presence. [7] The Stoic wisdom of Pleberio and the heightened consciousness of Melibea are again contrasted with Alisa's folly and lack of perception: «¿E piensas que sabe ella qué cosa sean hombres? ¿Si se casan o qué es casar?» (II. 151).

In Act XIX Melibea's consciousness, like Calisto's in Act XIV, finds poetic expression. Yet her imagination is linked with des-

---

[6] Cf. Vasurtus' edict on the inescapable facts of the matter —«nam cum nos sumus in esse permanenti et intellectus noster intelligat in instanti: cum affirmamus aliquid esse vel fuisse vel futurus esse: locutio nostra trahitur ad indiuisibile in quo sumus» (op. cit., fol. D3 recto).

[7] «L'amour romantique croit que l'absolu est atteint dans l'instant, et qu'il n'y a plus rien à attendre de l'avenir. Mais il se trompe... l'amour romantique ne s'intéresse qu'à la conquête; il ignore l'art de la possession durable où les sentiments mûrissent. Il faut plus de force et de talent pour conserver que pour acquérir» (Jean Pucelle, *Le Temps,* Paris, 1955, p. 98).

cription in the present, not with memory; nature is animated and mirrors human love in her description of the garden:

> Todo se goza este huerto con tu venida. Mira la luna quán clara se nos muestra, mira las nuues cómo huyen. Oye la corriente agua desta fontezica, ¡quánto más suaue murmurio y zurrío lleua por entre las frescas yeruas! Escucha los altos cipreses ¡cómo se dan paz unos ramos con otros por intercessión de vn templadico viento que los menea! (II. 180).

This is the climactic statement of the powers of consciousness as a positive force in *La Celestina*. Through the first nineteen acts memory has served as a vehicle for external description. Its fatal powers and its qualities of redemption have been examined. It has been redefined as all of consciousness and has worked in league with imagination. Now Rojas has moved to the last plateau; the external world has intruded on the present of consciousness, and imagination and the past have temporarily been deserted. Through Melibea the ideal world has momentarily been realized in the present; she has moved further than Calisto. But time and causality will prove inevitable; in the last two acts it is Pleberio, and not Melibea, who will have the final word.

In the *Tractado de Centurio*, descriptive memory also emerges in an objective and «novelistic» sense, and overtones of external description enter the present speech of the characters, as well as their memory. For example, Centurio is described by Areúsa when she berates him for cowardice — «Los cabellos crespos, la cara acuchillada, dos vezes açotado, manco de la mano del espada, treynta mugeres en la putería» (II. 133, Act XV). Similar portraits of Celestina had occurred only when she was being described from memory.

As for memory itself, Elicia recalls Celestina and describes her death in Act XV; these memories combine personal and objective reminiscence. Celestina is at first remembered by Elicia only as the *alcahuetas* presence benefited the girl — «aquélla que yo tenía por madre, aquélla que me regalaua, aquélla que me encubría, aquélla con quien yo me honrraua entre mis yguales, aquélla por quien yo era conocida en toda la ciudad e arrabales» (II. 135). But later she regrets her mistreatment of Celestina, and recalls the *alcahueta*'s warning that Elicia's laziness would lead to her downfall after Celestina was gone — « ¡O Celestina sabia, honrrada y autorizada, quántas faltas no encobrías con tu buen saber! Tú trabajauas, yo holgaua; tú salías fuera, yo estaua encerrada; tú rota, yo vestida; tú entrauas contino como abeja por casa, yo destruya, que otra cosa no sabía hazer» (II. 138-139). Elicia's laments are parallel, both in style and content, to Celestina's remorse over the loss of Claudina.

However, in her description of Celestina's death, Elicia's sorrow is tempered by a sense of fairness. She not only describes but tries to enter the mental processes of Sempronio and Pármeno, to give the human as well as the external version of the fight — they were «muy ayrados de no sé qué questiones que dizen que auían auido»; Celestina answered their demand for the gold chain «aun descubriendo otras cosillas de secretos»; the young men finally became «muy enojados, por vna parte los aquexaua la necessidad, que priua todo amor; por otra, el enojo grande e cansancio que trayan, que acarrea alteración; por otra, auían la fe quebrada de su mayor esperança» (II. 136-137). This reminds one of Sosia's earlier attempt to describe the sufferings of the condemned servants not only from his point of view but from theirs as well (II. 108-110, Act XIII). Thus a sense of objectivity is injected into descriptive memory. Elicia does not manipulate the facts for her own advantage; rather, the voice of the author seems to be breaking through, recapitulating the exact action of Act XII. The human drama is infused with a «novelistic» technique.

Areúsa then proceeds to take up the role left vacant by Sempronio's death. She becomes the champion of forgetfulness — «Con nueuo amor oluidarás los viejos. Vn hijo que nasce restaura la falta de tres finados: con nueuo sucessor se pierde la alegre memoria e plazeres perdidos del passado» (II. 141). Elicia practises the forgetfulness which Sempronio had preached, for in Act XVII she takes Areúsa's advice and puts aside her mourning; the memory of Celestina is doing her more harm than good. «Ya no veo las músicas de la aluorada, ya no las canciones de mis amigos, ya no las cuchilladas ni ruydos de noche por mi causa e, lo que peor siento, que ni blanca ni presente veo entrar por mi puerta» (II. 153). Even Celestina is forgotten after her death; *oluido* envelops the characters of *La Celestina*. [8]

---

[8] An interesting parallel is that realization of modern anonymity which will be one of the hallmarks of the modern novel. Speaking of Dickens, Donald Fanger notes that «the sinister side of that urban anonymity which so attracts Oliver Twist at first is already spelled out in 'Thoughts about People', which begins by

The attack on Calisto, masterminded by Areúsa, is undertaken more for envy of Melibea (as Tristán points out in Act XIX) than to revenge the forgotten lovers and *alcahueta*. But Areúsa has learned a few tricks from Celestina; she extorts from the naive Sosia the news of Calisto's scheduled evening visit to Melibea («me dexes en la memoria los días que aueys concertado de salir», II. 161, Act XVII), and exults that «otra arte es ésta que la de Celestina; avnque ella me tenía por boua, porque me quería yo serlo» (II. 162-163). The acute pride, self-consciousness, and isolation of Areúsa, already evident in the banquet scene («me viuo sobre mí») have developed into a fierce ill-will and envy diametrically opposed to the «después que a mí me sé conoscer» of Melibea. The *oluido* which she embraces and forces on the weaker Elicia is the logical ending of her trajectory of solitude. [9] And Rojas' irony has been turned against his own formula for escape. The forgetfulness which isolates the lovers from time and bridges the years to link the aged with their remote, happier past, becomes the forgetfulness of death, a forgetfulness which envelops even Celestina herself.

The final sparks of memory in the *Tractado de Centurio* are provided by Centurio himself. This rather misplaced character (who probably owes his existence as much to the *rufián* and *labrador* figures just emerging in the primitive Spanish drama, as to the classic *miles gloriosus*). [10] is the only character in *La Celestina* to provide a total objective background for his own existence; he is nevertheless the most two-dimensional character in the work. He regales his listeners with a minute description of his bare living quarters — «En vna casa biuo qual vees, que rodará el majadero por toda ella sin que

observing: 'It is strange with how little notice, good, bad, or indifferent, a man may live and die in London. He awakes no sympathy in the breast of any single person; his existence is a matter of interest to no one save himself; he cannot be said to be forgotten when he dies, for no one remembered him when he was alive'» *(Dostoevsky and Romantic Realism,* Cambridge, Mass., 1965, pp. 78-79).

[9] Contrary to my analysis, a number of critics see Areúsa as a discontinuous character: María Rosa Lida de Malkiel, for example, believes that the original Elicia and Areúsa switch rôles in the additional acts *(Originalidad,* pp. 662-676).

[10] María Rosa Lida de Malkiel discusses the sources and imitations of Centurio at length *(Originalidad,* 702-720), although she does not mention the contemporary theater of Juan del Encina and Lucas Fernández and its relations with Centurio. For example, in Fernández' *Egloga o Farsa del nascimiento de Nuestro Redemptor Jesucristo,* the shepherd Bonifacio is a braggart of the same sort as Centurio: «Entra primero Bonifacio alabándose y jactándose de ser zagal muy sabido y muy polido y esforzado, y mañoso y de buen linaje» (in *Farsas y églogas al modo y estilo pastoril y castellano;* ed. M. Cañete, RAE, Madrid, 1867, pp. 139-141).

tropiece. Las alhajas que tengo es el axuar de la frontera, vn jarro desbocado, vn assador sin punta. La cama en que me acuesto está armada sobre aros de broqueles, vn rimero de malla rota por colchones, vna talega de dados por almohada» (II. 166, Act. XVIII). He also gives a comic genealogy:

> CENTURIO: Por ella le dieron Centurio por nombre a mi abuelo e Centurio se llamó mi padre e Centurio me llamo yo.
> ELICIA: Pues ¿qué hizo el espada por que ganó tu abuelo esse nombre? Dime, ¿por ventura fue por ella capitán de cient hombres?
> CENTURIO: No; pero fue rufián de cient mugeres (II. 169). [11]

Rojas is somewhat heavy-handed with the persona of Centurio — althought he even has a family tree, the character is as exaggerated on the objective side as the other characters are on the subjective.

Yet Centurio the coward is not entirely devoid of character value. His contribution is to add a new dimension to that kind of imagined bravery discovered by Sempronio and Pármeno. Centurio's world of bravery does not have the slightest basis in fact; rather it is based on the world of imagination and dreams. «La noche passada soñaua que hazía armas en vn desafío por su seruicio con quatro hombres que ella bien conosce, e maté al vno» (II. 167).

To summarize, Rojas further develops, in the additional acts, the tendencies of memory to expand and give an extra dimension of

---

[11] Commenting on this passage Gilman notes that «the trajectory is that of the joke externally generated —the remark directed to the reader and intended for his laughter» (*Art.*, p. 203). Tristán also gives Sosia's peasant genealogy: «Ya sabrá que te llaman Sosia e a tu padre llamaron Sosia, nascido e criado en vna aldea, quebrando terrones con vn arado, para lo qual eres tú más dispuesto que para enamorado» (II, 175, Act XIX). The comic genealogies had already entered the world of the theater, and would enter the novel with the continuations of *La Celestina* and the *Lazarillo*. For example, Encina's first *Egloga representada en la noche de natividad* contains this exchange:

> MATEO: ¡Oh Juan, Juan, hi de Pascuala!
> Cata, cata, ¿acá estás tú?
> JUAN: Digo, digo, pues ¿qué hu?
> ¿Has de haber tú ell alcabala?
> MATEO: ¿Ya tú presumes de gala,
> Que te arrojas al palacio?
> ¡Andar mucho enhoramala!
> ¿Cuidas que eres para en sala?
> No te vien de gerenacio.

(*Teatro completo*, ed. F. Asenjo Barbieri, RAE, Madrid, 1893, p. 5).

65

freedom and imagination to the characters. Conversely he reinforces the inescapable fact of human insignificance and helplessness. But, as memory has functioned to express the inner man, the external use of memory to provide third-person narration begins to disappear, and descriptions suddenly move into the present. A new character, Centurio, enjoys such a well-documented existence in the present that he becomes more caricature than character. His reality is aimed externally; there is no inner being to reveal. Centurio is a character who has wandered into *La Celestina* from the drama.

B. «LA CELESTINA» AS LITERARY PRECEDENT.

Recapitulating, therefore, the generic conclusions of the previous chapters, we have seen that Rojas is the first Spanish author to use memory as that point at which the external and internal lives of his characters meet. In the additional acts the use of memory to heighten the subjective realities of the characters is intensified, but the objective function of memory begins to dissolve and to be replaced by an external description akin to dramatic exposition. Several of these tendencies in the additional acts will in turn be inherited by the continuations of *La Celestina.*

The continuations fall into two main categories — the dialogue sentimental novel (*Thebayda,* for example), [12] and the theatrical continuations (*Segunda Celestina*). [13] The former learned little from *La Celestina* about the use of memory. Rather, they revert to the commonplace stylizations of the sentimental novel. Lovers' oblivion is a favorite topic with the *Comedia Thebayda;* (BERINTO: «Espantado estoy, y aora conosco quán ageno me hallo dela verdad, y quán oluidado estoy de mí mesmo. ¿Y cómo ay estáuades vosotros y no os veya?», fol. iii verso, p. 11). *La Thebayda* also stresses the Petrarchan and Stoic idea of memory as a defense (GALTERIO: «¡Qué memoria tiene el diablo! Siempre lo oy afirmar y aora lo tengo por más cierto que no ay hombre tan loco que no se acuerde delas cosas que más

---

[12] I have used the 1521 edition (Valencia: George Costilla) which includes the *Thebayda,* the *Ypolita,* and the *Serafina,* with cross-references to and punctuation from the recent edition of *La comedia Thebaida,* by G. D. Trotter and Keith Whinnom (London, Colección Támesis, 1969).

[13] Feliciano de Silva, *Segunda comedia de Celestina* (Medina del Campo: Pedro Touans, 1534).

le empeçen», fol. iv recto, p. 13). But these assertions never transcend the level of the commonplace; memory never attains a crucial rôle in *La Thebayda* or in the continuations of its ilk.

The more «dramatic» continuations do follow the lead of *La Celestina,* but only that of the twenty-one act version. Memory becomes the servant of theatrical exposition and comic relief:

> PANDULPHO: Di ¿tú no conoces a Mostafas el carnicero?
> SIGERIL: Sí conosco mas ¿para qué es agora esso?
> PANDULPHO: Para que sepas lo que passé con él ayer en casa de Silea la cantora.
> SIGERIL: ¿Qué passaste?
> PANDULPHO: Pregunta lo tú a Barañón el moço de cauallos que él te lo dirá: porque no es bien los hombres dezir sus cosas (*Segunda Celestina,* fol. Aiv verso).

It is not until the advent of the picaresque novel that *La Celestina*'s use of memory seems to have had any tangible influence on generic progress, but in the *Lazarillo* some direct influences are visible. Claudio Guillén has already analysed «la disposición temporal del *Lazarillo de Tormes*» and has reached a number of conclusions about the function of memory in the work:

> El proceso de selección a que Lázaro somete su existencia nos muestra aquello que le importa manifestar: los rasgos fundamentales de su persona. Los puntos culminantes de la obra coinciden con unos hechos de conciencia: con los componentes esenciales de la memoria de Lázaro. Situados y contemplados en el plano de la conciencia, en el presente, los acontecimientos no dan lugar a huecos o interrupciones. Todo sucede, por lo tanto, como si una memoria, penetrando en sí misma, sacase a la superficie unos elementos básicos y *luego* los desenvolviese en el tiempo, a lo largo de una duración unilinear... La relación que Lázaro escribe consiste, pues, en un ir desplegando o «desarrollando» aquello que él sabe forma parte de su vivir y su ser actuales. La forma de la novela es *la «proyección»* —o, mejor dicho, autoproyección— *de la persona en el tiempo*. No sólo desde el presente, sino con él, se construye un pasado [14].

The *Lazarillo* has learned to use memory as a complete external and internal vision of human life, and *La Celestina*'s use of this tech-

[14] *HR* XXV (1957), 271-272.

nique in memory passages has been expanded by an unknown author.

The influence of *La Celestina* on the *Lazarillo* is incontestable. The rememberer, Pármeno, is a direct antecedent of the rememberer, Lázaro. Pármeno's negative memories in Act I — «Señor, yua a la plaça e trayale de comer e acompañáuala; suplía en aquellos menesteres, que mi tierna fuerça bastaua» (I. 69); «Avnque soy moço, cosas he visto asaz e el seso e la vista de las muchas cosas demuestran la experiencia» (I. 89); «E algunas vezes, avnque era niño, me subías a la cabeçera e me apretauas contigo e porque olías a vieja, me fuya de ti» (I. 99). All these suggest Lazarillo's first hint of the degradation which was his birthright — «Y allí, padeciendo mil importunidades, se acabó de criar mi hermanico, hasta que supo andar, y a mí hasta ser buen mozuelo, que iba a los huéspedes por vino y candelas y por lo demás, que me mandaban.» [15]

But the memory parallels become even more specific. Lazarillo's ironic use of *oluido* is announced in the very first words of the prologue: «Yo por bien tengo que cosas tan señaladas, y por ventura nunca oídas ni vistas, vengan a noticia de muchos y no se entierren en la sepultura del olvido, pues podría ser que alguno que las lea halle algo que le agrade, y a los que no ahondaren tanto los deleyte» (p. 3). The author's irony in rescuing these events from the «sepultura del oluido», is all the more obvious since he himself remains anonymous. And it is the insignificance of Lázaro's life, not its importance, which will be sung by the author. Rojas' sense of irony about human insignificance is carried over into the *Lazarillo*.

There are also specific reminiscences in the *Lazarillo* which obviously have their origin in *La Celestina*. For example, a vision of Celestina in her social milieu will be transformed by the *Lazarillo* into a comment on hunger, for once satiated:

En los conbites, en las fiestas, en las bodas, en las cofadrías, en los mortuorios, en todos los ayuntamientos de gentes, con ella pasan tiempo. (I. 68, Act I)	Mas el lacerado mentía falsamente, porque en cofradías y mortuorios que rezamos, a costa ajena comía como lobo y bebía más que un saludador. (p. 19)

This negative obsession with food and taste, which had been foreshadowed by Celestina's hedonism («que, avnque tengo la dife-

---

[15] *La vida de Lazarillo de Tormes,* ed. R. O. Jones (Manchester, 1963), p. 6.

rencia de los gustos e sabor en la boca, no tengo la diuersidad de sus tierras en la memoria») is, according to Lukács, one of the distinctive marks of the novel. [16]

In short, therefore, memory in the *Lazarillo* becomes only a weapon against the world, a metaphor for consciousness as a defense. It is as though Pármeno had been allowed in *La Celestina* to become the main rememberer: «Y en cuanto esto pasaba, a la memoria me vino una cobardía y flojedad que hice, por que me maldecía, y fue no dejalle sin narices, pues tan buen tiempo tuve para ello que la meitad del camino estaba andado... Pluguiera a Dios que lo hubiera hecho, que eso fuera así que así» (p. 14). The only exception to this rule is the interlude with the *escudero* — «Bebimos, y muy contentos nos fuimos a dormir como la noche pasada» (p. 36). The idea of human communion takes over, as it did in memory in *La Celestina* — «juntas comíamos, juntas dormíamos, juntas auíamos nuestros solazes...» (I. 134, Act III). For a short time Lázaro escapes the inevitable world of defensive memory, and enjoys the evasion which Celestina practised through the memory of companionship.

The final point of contact between the two worlds of the *Lazarillo* and *La Celestina* has been expressed by Guillén — «Así como Lázaro vive de día en día, de instante en instante, su memoria va atesorando las lecciones del pasado, y su voluntad le mantiene en tensión continua hacia el futuro» (*art. cit.,* p. 277). Rojas' intuition of human consciousness as the confrontation of three times, present, past, and future, has been fully elaborated in the *Lazarillo*. As a complete act of memory, this picaresque novel not only uses Rojas' solution to the problems of expressing both internal duration and external dimension, but gives this solution a coherent narrative form by choosing the autobiographical method first suggested by *La Celestina.* [17]

---

[16] «Takt und Geschmack, an und für sich untergeordnete Kategorien, die durchaus der blossen Lebenssphäre angehören und selbst einer wesentlichen ethischen Welt gegenüber belanglos sind, gewinnen hier eine grosse und konstitutive Bedeutung: bloss durch sie ist die Subjektivität von Anfang und Abschluss der Romantotalität imstande, sich im Gleichgewicht zu halten, sich als episch normative Objektivität zu setzen und so die Abstraktheit, die Gefahr dieser Form, zu überwinden» (*Die Theorie,* p. 72).

[17] This concern with autobiographical memory, and the influence of *La Celestina,* do not stop with the *Lazarillo*. George Haley has already analysed «Chronology and Structure» in his study of *Vicente Espinel and Marcos de Obregón* (Providence, 1959), pp. 101-119. He points out Vicente Espinel's concern with the

The idea of memory as the meeting point of the subjective and objective worlds will burst forth on the universal plane in the eighteenth century with Sterne's *Tristram Shandy,* long considered the pioneer of the modern novel's use of Bergsonian *durée.* [18] This study of memory in *La Celestina* has, I hope, established that the roots of this supposedly modern development extend at least back to late fifteenth-century interpretations of Aristotelian time, and find a clear antecedent in *La Celestina.* Aristotle's temporal theories, so often placed by critics in opposition to contemporary ideas of duration in the novel, [19] in fact sow the seed of Rojas' development of memory as the symbol of time-consciousness, and his concept of human life as the meeting point of present, past, and future. Aristotle also holds the clue to Rojas' seemingly contradictory time planes, for the idea of time as motion implies the necessity of sampling internal duration, a sampling which need not coincide with external dimension. If time often seems out of joint in *La Celestina,* it is because for Rojas, time and space are equivalent to motion, and all are joined in memory.

---

workings of artificial memory; the relativity of temporal notions, and chronological relationships:

> Names, events, impressions crowd upon the present demanding to be recorded, having been set free from the past by a word, a scene, a taste, a person. The discursive quality of much of the novel can be attributed to the workings of what would today be called involuntary memory (p. 114).

The relativism in memory is stressed even further by Mateo Alemán:

> Común y general costumbre ha sido y es de los hombres, cuando les pedís reciten y refieran lo que oyeron o vieron, o que os digan la verdad y sustancia de una cosa, enmascaralla y afeitalla, que se desconoce como el rostro de la fea. Cada uno le da sus matices y sentidos, ya para exagerar, incitar, aniquilar o divertir, según su pasión le dita (*Guzmán de Alfarache,* ed. Samuel Gili y Gaya, 5 vols., Clásicos Castellanos, Madrid, 1926, I. 52).

[18] See for example A. A. Mendilow, *Time and the Novel* (London, 1952, pp. 145-156).

[19] Lukács makes this mistake; for him the temporal unities of the classical drama are «Aristotelian» (*Die Theorie,* p. 130). This cliché has precluded further investigation of Aristotle's theories of time.

LIST OF WORKS CITED

AGUIRRE, J. M.: *Calisto y Melibea, amantes cortesanos.* Zaragoza, 1962.

ALEMÁN, Mateo: *Guzmán de Alfarache,* ed. Samuel Gili y Gaya, 5 vols. Madrid, 1926.

ALONSO, Dámaso: *De los siglos oscuros al de oro.* Madrid, 1958.

ASENSIO, Manuel: «El tiempo en *La Celestina,*» *HR,* XX (1952),28-43.

— «El tiempo y el género literario en *La Celestina,*» *RFH,* VII (1945), 147-157.

BATAILLON, Marcel: *La Célestine selon Fernando de Rojas.* Paris, 1961.

CASTRO, Américo: *La Celestina como contienda literaria.* Madrid, 1965.

— *La realidad histórica de España.* México D. F., 1954.

CASTRO GUISASOLA, F.: *Observaciones sobre las fuentes literarias de La Celestina. RFE.* Anejo V. Madrid, 1924.

COLUMNA, Guido de: *Crónica Troyana.* Pamplona: Arnalt Guillén de Brocar, 1500.

CRAIG, Hardin: «The Shackling of Accidents: A Study of Elizabethar Tragedy,» *PQ,* XIX (1940), 1-19.

CRIADO DE VAL, M.: *Indice verbal de La Celestina. RFE.* Anejo LXIV. Madrid, 1955.

CURTIUS, E. R.: *European Literature and the Latin Middle Ages.* New York, 1963.

DEYERMOND, A. D.: *The Petrarchan Sources of La Celestina.* Oxford, 1961.

ENCINA, Juan del: *Teatro completo,* ed. F. Asenjo Barbieri. RAE. Madrid, 1893.

ERASMUS, Desiderius: *La lengua de Erasmo roterodamo...,* n. p., 1533.

— *Lingua.* [Nurenberg], 1525.

FANGER, Donald: *Dostoevsky and Romantic Realism.* Harvard Studies in Comparative Literature, n. 27, Cambridge, Mass., 1965.

FERNÁNDEZ, Lucas: *Farsas y églogas al modo y estilo pastoril y castellano.* Ed. M. Cañete. RAE. Madrid, 1867.

FERNANDEZ, Ramón: *Messages.* Paris, 1926.

FLORES, Juan de: *Breve tractado de Grimalte y Gradissa.* [Lérida, 1495?]. Facsim. RAE. Madrid, 1954.

— *Grisel y Mirabella*. [Lérida, 1495?]. Facsim. RAE. Madrid, 1954.

GILMAN, Stephen: «A propos of 'El tiempo en *La Celestina*' by Manuel J. Asensio», *HR*, XXI (1953), 42-45.

— «Fernando de Rojas as Author», *RF*, LXXVI (1964), 255-290.

— «Rebirth of a Classic: Celestina» in *Varieties of Literary Experience*, ed. Stanley Burnshaw. New York, 1962, pp. 283-305.

— *The Art of La Celestina*. Madison, Wisconsin, 1956.

— «The Death of Lazarillo de Tormes», *PMLA*, LXXXI (1966), 149-166.

— «The Imperfect Tense in the *Poema del Cid*», *Comparative Literature*, VIII (1956), 291-306.

GILMAN, Stephen, and Ruggerio, Michael: «Rodrigo de Reinosa and *La Celestina*», *RF*, LXXIII (1961), 255-284.

GILMAN, Stephen, and Valle Lersundi, F. del: «Mollejas el ortelano» in *Estudios dedicados a James Homer Herriott*. Madison, 1966.

GREEN, Otis H.: «On Rojas' Description of Melibea», *HR*, XIV (1946), 254-256.

— *Spain and the Western Tradition*, I. Madison, 1963.

GUILLÉN, Claudio: «La disposición temporal del *Lazarillo de Tormes*», *HR*, XXV (1957), 264-279.

GYBBON-MONYPENNY, G. B.: «Autobiography in the *Libro de Buen Amor* in the Light of some Literary Comparisons, *BHS*, XXIV (1957), 63-78.

HALEY, George: *Vicente Espinel and Marcos de Obregón. A Life and its Literary Representation*. Brown University Studies. Vol. XXV. Providence, 1959.

HOLTON, Gerald: «Science and the Changing Allegory of Motion», *Scientia* XCVIII (1963), 191-200.

KOYRÉ, Alexandre: «Galileo and Plato», *Journal of the History of Ideas*, IV (1943), 400-428.

La vida del Lazarillo de Tormes, ed. R. O. Jones. Manchester, 1963.

LEWIS, C. S.: *The Discarded Image*. Cambridge, Eng., 1964.

LIDA DE MALKIEL, María Rosa: *La originalidad artística de La Celestina*. Buenos Aires, 1962.

LÓPEZ DE VILLALOBOS, Francisco: *Algunas obras de—*. Ed. Antonio María Fabié. SBE 24. Madrid, 1886.

LUKÁCS, Georg: *Die Theorie des Romans*. Berlin: Spandau, 1963.

MAEZTU, Ramiro de: *Don Quijote, Don Juan y la Celestina*. Madrid, 1926.

MAIMONIDES, Moses: *The Guide for the Perplexed*, trans. M. Friedlander. New York, 1956.

MATULKA, Barbara: *The Novels of Juan de Flores and their European Diffusion*. New York, 1931.

MENDILOW, A. A.: *Time and the Novel*. London, 1952.

MENÉNDEZ Y PELAYO, Marcelino: «La Celestina» in *Orígenes de la novela*. III. (Edición nacional XV). Madrid (Santander), 1943.

MUIR, Edwin: *The Structure of the Novel*. London, 1928.

NORTON, F. J.: *Printing in Spain 1501-1520*. Cambridge, Eng., 1966.

PADRÓN, Juan del: *Obras de Juan Rodríguez de la Cámara (o del Padrón)*. SBE 22, ed. Antonio Paz y Melia. Madrid, 1884.

PENNEY, Clara Louisa: *The book called Celestina...* New York, 1954.

PETRARCA, Francesco: *Clarissimi de Remediis utriusque fortunae: ad Azonam*. Cremona, 1492.

— *De los remedios contra prospera y aduersa fortuna*. Valladolid: Diego de Gumiel, 1510.

PUCELLE, Jean: *Le Temps*. Paris, 1955.

RIQUER, Martín de: «Fernando de Rojas y el primer acto de 'La Celestina'», *RFE*, XLI (1957), 373-395.

ROJAS, Fernando de: *La Celestina*, ed. Julio Cejador y Frauca. Madrid, 1962; first ed. 1910.

— *La Celestina*, ed. M. Criado de Val and G. D. Trotter. Madrid, 1958.

— *La Celestina*, intro. Stephen Gilman, ed. Dorothy S. Severin. Madrid, 1969.

SAN PEDRO, Diego de: *Obras*, ed. Samuel Gili y Gaya. Madrid, 1950.

SILVA, Feliciano de: *Segunda comedia de Celestina*. Medina del Campo: Pedro Touans, 1534.

SIMÓN DÍAZ, J.: *Bibliografía de la literatura hispánica*, III, 2nd ed., vol. II, Madrid, 1965.

SPITZER, Leo: *Sobre antigua poesía española*. Buenos Aires, 1962.

SYLVIUS, Aeneas: *Historia de dos amantes*. Seville: Jacobo Cromberger, 1512.

TEIXIDOR, Laurent: *Observations sur La Celestina*. Périgueux, 1968.

Comedia Theybayda... Valencia: George Costilla, 1521.

THIBAUDET, Albert: *Réflexions sur le roman*. Paris, 1938.

TORNER, E. M.: *Lírica hispánica*. Madrid, 1966.

TORRE, Alfonso de la: «Visión delectable de la filosofía y de las artes liberales...», ed. Adolfo de Castro in *Curiosidades bibliográficas*. BAE 36. Madrid, 1855.

TROTTER, G. D.: «The 'Coplas de las comadres' of Rodrigo de Reynosa and 'La Celestina'» in *Homenaje a Dámaso Alonso*. Madrid, 1963, III, 527-537.

— and Whinnom, Keith: *La comedia Thebaida*, London, 1969.

VALLE LERSUNDI, F. del: «Testamento de Fernando de Rojas, autor de 'La Celestina'», *RFE*, XVI (1929), 366-388.

VASURTO, Rodrigo: *De natura loci et temporis*. Salamanca, 1494.

VIVES, Juan Luis: *De anima et vita*. Basel, 1538.

— *Diálogos latinos de...*, ed. C. Fernández. Barcelona, 1940.

YATES, Frances A.: «The Ciceronian Art of Memory» in *Medioevo e Rinascimento. Studi in onore di Bruno Nardi*. Florence, 1955, II, 871-903.

— *The Art of Memory*. London, 1966.

ZÁRATE, Fray Hernando de: «Discursos de la paciencia cristiana», in *Escritores del siglo XVI*. BAE 27. Madrid, 1853, pp. 419-684.

COLECCION TAMESIS

SERIE A - MONOGRAFIAS

SERIE B - TEXTOS

El sufrimiento premiado. Comedia famosa, atribuida en esta edición, por primera vez, a Lope de Vega Carpio. Introducción y notas de V. F. Dixon, pp. xxvii + 177.

José de Cadalso: *Cartas marruecas.* Prólogo, edición y notas de Lucien Dupuis y Nigel Glendinning, pp. lxiii + 211.

Virgilio Malvezzi: *Historia de los primeros años del reinado de Felipe IV.* Edición y estudio preliminar por D. L. Shaw, pp. liv + 206, with 3 illustrations and 3 maps.

La comedia Thebaida. Edited by G. D. Trotter and Keith Whinnom, pp. lxi + 270.

Juan Vélez de Guevara: *Los celos hacen estrellas.* Editada por J. E. Varey y N. D. Shergold, con una edición de la música por Jack Sage, pp. cxvii + 277.

Francisco Bances Candamo: *Theatro de los theatros de los passados y presentes siglos.* Prólogo, edición y notas de Duncan W. Moir, pp. cii + 191.

Pedro Calderón de la Barca: *La hija del aire.* Edición crítica, con introducción y notas de Gwynne Edwards, pp. lxxxviii + 298.

SERIE D - REPRODUCCIONES EN FACSIMIL

Cayetano Alberto de la Barrera y Leirado: *Catálogo bibliográfico y biográfico del teatro antiguo español, desde sus orígenes hasta mediados del siglo XVIII (Madrid, 1860),* pp. xi + 727.

1103